TENNIS'S STRANGEST MATCHES

TENNIS'S STRANGEST MATCHES

Peter Seddon

ROBSON BOOKS

This edition published in Great Britain in 2001 by Robson Books,
The Chrysalis Building, Bramley Road, London W10 6SP

Reprinted in 2004, 2005

An imprint of **Chrysalis** Books Group plc

Copyright © 2001, 2004, 2005 Peter Seddon

British Library Cataloguing in Publication Data
A catalogue record for this title is available from the British Library

ISBN 1 86105 379 7

Typeset by SX Composing DTP, Rayleigh, Essex
Printed and bound in Great Britain by Creative Print &
Design (Wales), Ebbw Vale

Contents

Introduction

Admirers of lawn tennis have used many words to explain the game's special appeal. Back in the nineteenth century it was 'a splendid and healthful pursuit', and it has since been variously described as graceful, exciting, beautiful, thrilling, athletic, pulsating, remarkable, unrivalled and awesome. Sometimes it is all of these, and more, at once.

There is another small adjective, too, which so often seems to creep into the annals of tennis literature. We're talking 'strange'.

Selecting those matches and incidents that somehow depart from the norm has been a tremendously enjoyable task but inevitably a subjective one. I had to resist the temptation merely to cite great matches, of which there have been many, and instead have sought out incidents or representations of tennis which are remarkable in other ways.

As a result, tennis's strangest stories have many themes. There are tales of murder and suicide ('One Shot After Another'), interference from wildlife ('A Sting in the Tail') and unusual playing techniques ('Redl's Special Service'). There are others where weather proved the victor ('Disruptive Diane'), seemingly impossible comebacks ('A Champagne Moment') and occasions when officials took centre stage ('Dorothy's Nightmare').

There are tales of tennis played in the most trying conditions ('Arthur Keeps Cool'), others where handicaps were entirely self-inflicted ('Well Smashed, Sir!) and those which entered the record books for reasons of length rather than quality ('The Rally from Hell!').

Other strange stories defy categorization. There are the aristocrats who unknowingly played with obsolete court markings for fully 13 years ('The Wrong-shaped Court') and the rather eccentric academic who turned gamesmanship into an art form to help him win against better opposition ('Joad's Gambit').

Umpires, doctors and streakers all get in on the act, as too do stockings, shorts and knickers along with aeroplanes and helicopters, squirrels and dogs, and a sundry collection of vicars.

And not forgetting the players, for it is they who are at the heart of all the action, their strong personalities and diverse characters, as well as their extraordinary ability, coming through time and again in *Tennis's Strangest Matches*.

The tales involve many different nationalities, reflecting the game's worldwide appeal, and cover venues as diverse as Surbiton and Tallahassee, the Albert Hall and the Houston Astrodome. Naturally I have chosen many incidents from Wimbledon, the spiritual home of lawn tennis, but the United States is well represented, as too are France, Italy and Australia.

As for the timespan, the stories are evenly spread from 1877 to 2000 and I have also selected half a dozen or so from the era of Royal Tennis, the venerable ancestor of the lawn game. As an incidental result I hope that a reading of all the stories chronologically should give a potted history of the origins and development of tennis.

My research practice has been to return to original sources, in particular, contemporary newspaper accounts and reports from the specialist tennis press. I have steered clear of relying on players' reminiscences as anything more than a pointer – they play so many games in so many places that I quickly discovered their memories weren't always as reliable as their forehands.

Among the many sources consulted and libraries visited I must extend special thanks to the Kenneth Ritchie Wimbledon Library at The Wimbledon Lawn Tennis Museum, whose collection of tennis literature is mind-boggling in its coverage and is made so readily accessible to researchers.

I also acknowledge help from individuals who pointed me in the direction of interesting cases. Julie Bunyan, Richard Marshall, Ian Methven and Alick Seddon all came up with suggestions and special mention must go to Kate Ibbitson for taking time out of a very busy schedule to cast an eye over all the finished stories and make useful comments.

Finally, I would like to thank Jeremy Robson and his editorial team at Robson Books for embracing the idea of *Tennis's Strangest Matches* so enthusiastically and guiding it through to completion.

LOST BALLS COST HIM DEAR

PERTH, SCOTLAND, FEBRUARY 1437

James I of Scotland (1394–1437) loved nothing more than a game of Royal Tennis, venerable ancestor of the lawn tennis we know today. After all, the Scots had a great pedigree in the game, having played since the reign of Alexander III in the thirteenth century, even before this most healthy of pastimes was documented in England.

But, like every player before and since, James found that the balls had a life of their own and simply refused to go where he wanted them to. Now any wayward shot can be expensive but no one in tennis history knows that better than James I because for him it wasn't just the lost points or lost balls that cost him dear. It was something much more important than that!

It was his games at the Blackfriars Monastery in Perth that were especially troublesome. Those unruly balls would insist on finding their way into a small open sewage drain in the corner of his court.

Now we're not talking a pressurized canister of four here. We're looking at handmade craftsman jobs, individually sewn in cloth or white leather, stuffed with dog hair or even the human stuff and shipped in from France subject to heavy import tax. Expensive was the word and, being a good Scotsman, James liked to watch the royal purse.

Contemporary accounts tell us that 'whane he playd at tenys the ballis he plaid with oft ranne yn at that fowle hole, so he maid to let stop it hard with stone'. The sensible fellow had blocked up the troublesome drain.

When he wasn't playing tennis, James was reforming Scotland with a vengeance, keeping the turbulent Highlanders in order and making vigorous efforts to limit the power of the nobility. The nobs weren't at all happy about this and swore vengeance.

On the night of 20 February 1437 a band of at least eight assassins led by Sir Robert Graham broke into the royal apartments at Blackfriars, slew a page, Walter Straton, on the staircase and approached the king's room, where he was in the company of the queen and some of her attendants.

The royal party sought to bar the door but a traitorous member of the court had removed the bolts. The king tried the windows but found them strongly barred. Seizing an iron poker from the fireplace he prised up a plank in the floor and lowered himself into 'thordure of the privay', the drain of the lavatory.

Although rather corpulent, he knew he could wriggle down the channel and escape through the flue into the tennis court. That is, until he remembered he'd blocked it up just days before. Trapped in the stinking hole he waited until his pursuers had searched and left the room before asking the ladies to lower down sheets to pull him out.

In a scene of tragic farce, which Laurel and Hardy would surely be proud of, lady-in-waiting Elizabeth Douglas over-reached and fell down the hole. The commotion brought the gang hurtling back up the stairs and King James, unarmed, was stabbed to death with swords and daggers after putting up a stout fight.

At only 43 he surely had many happy years of tennis ahead of him but wayward shots, lost balls, a canny head and a wheelbarrow full of rubble had cost him dear.

Many players have seen their chances of winning a vital match disappear down the pan, but this is the only known case in tennis-match history when loss of balls have led to loss of life!

IT'S A BLOOMIN' RACKET!

WINDSOR CASTLE, JANUARY 1506

There's nothing worse than feeling technologically challenged by an opponent who steals a march in the matter of equipment. How many club players must have turned up for games in the 1970s clutching a trusty wooden-framed Dunlop Maxply Fort only for their hearts to sink as they saw their opponent wielding a metal-framed Prince Classic 'Jumbo' resembling a snow shoe? Disheartening is the word.

But no player in history has suffered such indignity as the Lord Marquis of Dorset who, at Windsor Castle on 31 January 1506, was duped in the most outrageous way possible.

He was entitled to expect better from his opponent, Philip, Archduke of Austria and King of Castille. Philip was, after all, being royally entertained by King Henry VII at his modest Windsor edifice, and ought surely to have 'played the game' in true English style.

But even 500 years ago, tennis technology was on the march and thereby lay the problem. Dorset, and indeed the rest of Tudor England at that time, played Court Tennis as the French and other Europeans had taught them, as *jeu de paume*, with the palm of the hand.

But towards the end of the fifteenth century, the devious continentals had gone and invented the tennis racket. And unforgivably, by the start of the sixteenth century, no one seemed yet to have told the English.

Now the marquis was the sort of trusting chap who always

3

expected the obvious. He'd look forward to a custard cream or a brandy snap with all the relish the names implied. Offer him a suite at the Seaview Hotel and he wouldn't expect a poky room at the rear overlooking the dustbins. But then, as now, an Englishman's trust in people and etymological accuracy was often completely misplaced, as the chronicler of the Windsor débâcle confirms:

'Bothe Kyngs went to the Tennys playe and there played the Kyng of Casteele with the Lord Marques of Dorset, Kyng Henry lookynge on them. But the Kyng of Casteele played with the rackete and gave the Lord Marques XV.'

It was, one supposes, decent of the Austro-Spanish monarch to agree to give the hapless Dorset a 15–love start but surely about as much use to the trusting marquis as a chocolate teapot.

Conveniently, it seems, Philip had omitted to pack a spare of the new-fangled implement and, thus deprived of the chance to borrow a racket, the resulting thrashing of the marquis was a foregone conclusion.

Never to be caught out again, the English kitted themselves out with a vengeance. Three years later, when a youthful, athletic and still slim Henry VIII succeeded his father as king of England the tennis-mad monarch wielded the racket with great skill and the royal inventory showed he had at least seven of them.

It is too late to comfort the gallant marquis of Dorset perhaps, unless he is yet nursing his swollen digits in the ethereal world of tennis somewhere on 'the other side', but it is worth noting that duplicity, in the long run, evidently doesn't pay.

No Austrian and only one Spanish representative, Mañuel Santana in 1966, has ever won the Wimbledon men's singles title. Despite a current and obviously temporary hiatus, British men have lifted the trophy on no fewer than 35 occasions.

Now there's justice for you.

CHARLES 'LE SUPERBRAT'

PALAIS DU LOUVRE, PARIS, AUGUST 1572

Bad behaviour on court and the problem of 'pushy' parents have contributed to the difficulties faced by more than a few of today's tennis stars. But even the modern-day traumas of France's Mary Pierce and Australia's Jelena Dokic, both of whom have suffered from famously disruptive fathers, pale into insignificance compared to those of King Charles IX of France (1550–74). In nearly 450 years of tennis history he remains unsurpassed when it comes to the age-old problems of 'court rage' and 'parental influence'.

Charles was a mad-keen enthusiast of Court Tennis at that time in the sixteenth century when every self-respecting royal in England and Europe had taken up the game. In fact he was the first child prodigy, having a miniature racket thrust into his hands at the age of two by his ambitious mother Catherine de Medici.

When he ascended the throne in 1560 he was only ten, and what ten-year-old boy wants to rule? Playing tennis is much more fun, and Charles pursued the game fervently into adulthood.

He might have known the game spelled trouble; his grandfather François I had died 13 years before Charles took the throne, having contracted a chill after overheating in a particularly vigorous match. It was a bad omen.

Charles's own infamous match took place on 22 August 1572 at the Louvre Royal Palace. He was 22, the same age as

'Mighty Mouth' John McEnroe when he was embellishing the English language with such immortal phrases as 'You cannot be serious' and 'Pits of the world'.

Coming into the game, Charles's biggest problem was his following camp. His Catholic mother Catherine was alarmed at his friendship with Admiral Coligny, political leader of the Protestant Huguenots. The two factions were, after all, at Civil War.

Matters bubbled up to a head and just after 10.30 am on 22 August someone took a pot shot at Coligny close to the tennis court in a failed attempt on his life. He immediately sent two messengers to inform his friend King Charles, who had just taken to the court with his partner the Duke of Guise for a men's doubles. A contemporary account relates the outcome: 'The messengers found the King in the tennis court and all witnesses agree on the spontaneous fury and bitterness with which he greeted the news: "Will I never have any peace?" he exclaimed. "Always new troubles." Then, throwing his racket to the ground he returned to the Palace.'

So it was 'Match abandoned, near death of friend'. Most inconsiderate and an obvious cue for racket-throwing. Further cue for entry of 'pushy mother'. She advised her son to put such disruptive friendships aside and finish off the troublesome Huguenots once and for all. It was a classic case of 'mother knows best'.

Two days later, in the most drastic case of post-match pique ever recorded, Charles ordered the St Bartholomew's Day Massacre of the Huguenots. Coligny and his fellow Protestant leaders were killed along with 4,000 others in Paris alone.

Charles played his last game of tennis just two years later, dying, aged only 24. His place in French history is assured. So too is his place in tennis history as 'Le Superbrat' of all time.

SHAKESPEARE'S GAME?

LONDON, SEPTEMBER 1579

When the Earl of Oxford and his playing partner approached the tennis court at their favourite palace one fine September day in the year of Queen Elizabeth 1579, they found to their chagrin it was already occupied by one Philip Sidney and another.

Sidney refused to budge.

'But my friend and I have the court appointed for this hour,' argued the young earl. A verbal spat ensued in which acid wit almost gave way to fisticuffs before the Earl of Oxford prevailed and a humbled but fuming Sidney left the court.

The finer details of the game which Edward de Vere, 17th Earl of Oxford, then embarked upon have been lost in the mists of time. Where, then, is the required peculiarity factor of this match? Curious, yes, as possibly the earliest ever 'this is our court, mate' impasse, but surely there is nothing more.

In fact there is a lot more. This is the only tennis match in history to become the centre of a literary mystery in which intrigue and petty squabbling have become commonplace, eminent academics discredited and the very foundations of English literature shaken to the core. We're talking the greatest literary conundrum of all time. I give you the immortal bard, Mr William Shakespeare.

The basis of the puzzle is simple. While most people accept that William Shakespeare of Stratford, he of the pointy beard and receding hairline, actually completed his works by his own hand, there are many scholars who disagree.

'Someone else wrote them,' they argue.

Prime candidate was the statesman and philosopher Francis Bacon, claimed Sir Edwin Durning-Lawrence in his 1910 blockbuster *Bacon is Shakespeare*. Had he written *Shakespeare is Ham* instead he might have found more support. The Baconian and Stratfordian factions still fight it out today.

There are other claimants too. The actor Richard Burbage, literary giants Ben Jonson, Christopher Marlowe and Edmund Spenser, Queen Elizabeth I, Mary Queen of Scots, Pope Adrian IV (otherwise known as Englishman Nicholas Brakespear), have all been put forward as prime candidates for 'the real Shakespeare' in what is known as 'The Authorship Question'.

But chief claimant of all time, say some, is our tennis-playing tyrant, the Earl of Oxford. 'Bunkum,' say others. But the Oxfordite theorists, like the earl himself, are not readily deterred. And they have used the 'Tennis Court Incident', as it is now known in Shakespearian research circles, as their 'proof' that Oxford was the real bard and Shakespeare of Stratford just an ordinary fellow.

The logic is simple enough. A number of well-observed references to tennis in Shakespeare's works prove he was an aficionado of the game. Yet exhaustive research into Shakespeare of Stratford's life has shown no evidence whatsoever of an interest in tennis; therefore he could not have written the works.

But the Earl of Oxford *was* a keen player, as 'the incident' proves conclusively. That in turn lends massive weight to the theory that Oxford *was* Shakespeare!

'Q.E.D.,' crow the Oxfordite lobby.

The logic may be stunning but it is also stunningly illogical. I once proved beyond all measure of doubt that my local side Burton Albion are a better football team than Manchester United by using a similar cumulative formula.

Nevertheless, that the playing of a single tennis match should be held up as evidence in such a controversial question surely secures its place in the annals of tennis strangeness.

What is far less certain is the veracity of these literary claims. Oxford did, after all, die in 1604, when several of Shakespeare's works had yet to be written!

It's a pity we can't ask the man who kickstarted the whole Oxford theory with his book *Shakespeare Identified*, published in 1920, to explain that little hiccup. He was a Gateshead schoolteacher blessed with the unfortunate name of J. Thomas Looney.

No comment. Except, perchance, 'Game, set and match to Shakespeare of Stratford'?

PLAYING FOR DOUGH

NANTES, FRANCE, MARCH 1590

Henry IV of France (1553–1610) was just about as keen as it's possible to be when it came to a game of Royal Tennis. He was an any time, any place, anywhere man, always insisted on playing for money, and didn't like losing. Although the royal account books show that he did do, frequently.

Contemporary reports relate how he could carry on almost to dropping point, 'with his grey shoes, his shirt torn at the back tied in a dog-leg knot, not being able to get to the ball through tiredness, moaning that he felt like a stumbling donkey.'

In a life filled with interesting contests against Europe's noblest names it was his curious match against the humble bakers of Nantes that deserves its place in history for providing the most fiendishly cunning response to the loss of a match ever recorded.

Although not officially accepted as king by the whole of France until 1594, he travelled the length and breadth of the land in a royal manner long before that and issued proclamations at the drop of a hat. Or indeed a set. Or more particularly three.

Entering Nantes on 18 March 1590, the town paid homage to Henry, a contemporary chronicler relating that 'he refreshed himself and passed the time by playing tennis against the bakers of the town.'

It didn't go well. Despite wielding the baton with some

vigour Henry was beaten in each of three sets and handed over his money with marked reluctance. The rejoicing bread barons found themselves in the dough even on their day off.

As any habitual gambler would know, walking away without trying to repair the damage isn't an option. Henry crustily demanded a re-match but the bakers stood firm. 'We shall not give you your revenge as we agreed only to play a maximum of three sets,' they reasoned.

That sort of talk might be appropriate with a few mates on the public park but perhaps the master *boulangers* ought to have used their loaf before adopting that tone with a royal personage, especially one who was a known bad loser. They'd made a bloomer.

Henry left the tennis court determined that if he couldn't win his money back he'd ruin those blackguardly bakers once and for all.

The next day, before leaving Nantes, he issued a proclamation that henceforth the price of a small loaf would cost the equivalent of a penny-ha'penny.

It was a prohibitive price for the public to pay. Contemplating the inevitably plummeting sales and ensuing bread riots the bakers sought out His Majesty to beg pardon. They pleaded for his mercy, imploring him to 'take whatever revenge you wish, except on our bread'.

Henry IV must surely rank as the worst loser in the game, peevishly taking his crumb of comfort from the only bakers ever sorry that their bread had risen.

This match is also uniquely strange in providing the most opportunities for hopelessly weak puns centred around all things bready, for which I offer my profuse apologies.

A VERY BIG POINT

MURO TORTO, ROME, MAY 1606

'At Stockton on 5 July 1884 a ball in play struck a sparrow very much in earnest and killed it on the spot.' That little gem quoted from a splendid history of tennis published in 1903 is sometimes playfully cited as the first tennis-related death. In fact it probably is the first to have occurred during a rally itself but the annals of the game can reveal even darker deeds than ornithological death by misadventure.

In the game between Michelangelo Amerighi and his good friend Ranuccio Tomassoni in Rome on 29 May 1606 we're talking murder.

This was no marathon match on the red clay of the Foro Italico, but the crowds who have played every shot at the Italian Open there with the likes of local hero Adriano Panatta would surely have reached fever pitch over this one.

The Italians and tennis go back a long way. Two thousand years ago the Ancient Romans played several ball games, some similar to tennis, and by the sixteenth century, *rachetta*, a form of what we now know as Real Tennis, was a popular recreation. It was an Italian, Antonio Scaino, who wrote the first ever tennis book in 1555. Even Julius Caesar played tennis, Scaino tells us. That's a dubious one; we know he came and saw but whether he conquered remains unrecorded.

The problem with tennis when Amerighi played Tomassoni at the Muro Torto court was that there were a number of

12

different versions of the rules. Arguments over scoring were commonplace.

Tomassoni knew he was playing with a hothead, for away from the tennis court Amerighi's previous disciplinary record didn't read too well:

1600 – Beating up a work colleague.
1601 – Wounding a soldier.
1603 – Imprisoned for sundry offences.
1604 – Throwing a plate of artichokes in the face of a waiter and arrested for throwing stones at the Roman Guard.
1605 – Seized for misuse of arms and wounding a man in defence of his mistress.

Tomassoni might have expected fireworks. The artichoke incident, in particular, had petulance written all over it, never an endearing quality in a tennis player.

In the event, Tomassoni got rather more than a leguminous barrage. Following the inevitable scoring dispute, a violent quarrel and vicious brawl ensued. With a reported cry of 'See how this feels now!' Amerighi drew a knife and stabbed his opponent to death.

In that moment of madness, two lives were effectively 'lost', for Amerighi fled from Rome, himself wounded and feverish, in terror of the consequences of his act. A fugitive on the run, he reached Naples in 1607 and moved on to Malta, then Sicily.

Although he worked throughout these travels, a safe return to Rome was what Amerighi desired and for that he needed the personal pardon of the Pope. It proved a long battle in which he won, but never knew it.

Back in Naples in 1609 he was attacked and left for dead; in July 1610 he decided to sail to Rome to seek a personal pardon but missed a connection en route, the boat leaving without him but taking all his belongings.

Match point in the game of life came all too soon. After contracting malaria Amerighi died from pneumonia at Porto

Ercole on 18 July 1610. He was 37.

One single tennis point had dogged him for four years. Three days after his death a document granting him forgiveness arrived from Rome.

It is a curious tennis story, and one made even more so by the identity of its villain.

Tennis players are often described as 'artists' but for Amerighi this was more than a metaphor. For Amerighi was none other than 'Caravaggio', the most controversial and celebrated artist of seventeenth-century Italy.

Learned art historians are convinced that the innovatory 'dark' and rather sombre later style of this world-famous figure resulted from the mental turmoil he suffered following his flight from the tennis arena.

Commentators sometimes airily say, 'There is so much riding on this one point.' A life taken. A life ruined. The course of art history changed. The final point in the Amerighi v. Tomassoni match must surely be the 'biggest' in all tennis history.

STROLLING TO VICTORY

FONTAINEBLEAU, FRANCE, MAY 1827

When today's tennis superstars walk the few yards from locker room to court they are invariably accompanied by a phalanx of 'bodyguards' to render their journey a comfortable one. No such luxury was enjoyed by the Frenchman J. Edmund Barre, the greatest Real Tennis star of the nineteenth century who, in 1827, opted for an entirely self-imposed and rather more arduous approach to one of the most important challenge matches of his career.

Barre was born in Grenoble in 1802 at a time when tennis, traditionally the 'Sport of Kings', had become sufficiently popularized for paid professionals to earn a living from it, playing for the World Championship and in challenge and exhibition games which made their names known to a wide public following.

Barre was so talented that he held the World Championship from 1829 to 1862 when he finally succumbed, at the age of 60, to the 36-year-old Englishman Edmund Tomkins.

By all accounts Barre was a likeable fellow, described by one of his contemporaries as displaying 'a genial courtesy, a good-humoured chaff, an absence of highly tinted idealization of his own form and with a complete unwillingness to take any undue advantage of an inexperienced player'.

He was also, though, something of a lovable rascal and mischievous wag with a penchant for 'winner take all' money matches and unconventional betting challenges. When it came

15

to taking on the pretenders to his crown, 'Papa' Barre was game for anything. It was not unusual for him to take on two men at once and if things were going well to play the odd shot between his legs or with his racket handle. Then, as now, the public loved an entertainer.

The Comte de Reignac fancied his chance in a challenge match against Barre and agreed to receive a handicap peculiar to Real Tennis called 'touch no walls'. It was a severe handicap for Barre to give away, even as undisputed World Champion.

That match was played at Fontainebleau in 1826 and Barre took the honours, needling the humbled count with the mischievously delivered parting shot, 'Touch no walls, touch no money!'

When the count immediately fired back with a demand for a return, Barre's riposte was just as swift: '*Comte, je viendrai au mois de Mai prochain, et je vous ferai la même partie, et je m'engage à faire le chemin à pied de Paris à Fontainebleau.*'

The count accepted the wager. Barre had offered to take him on under the same handicap but also agreed to walk all the way from his Paris base to do so, a distance of 43 miles!

On 5 May 1827 Barre, then a cocksure 25-year-old and 'an athlete of more than ordinary calibre' started at daybreak and reached Paris less than 10 hours later.

After just an hour's rest he again faced the count and again 'touched no walls'. Suffice it to say the hapless count again 'touched no money'. The next day Barre cheerfully walked back to Paris accompanied by his equally unorthodox colleague Louis Labbé, who once played an entire match carrying a man on his back.

And they weren't the only tennis professionals with a penchant for such freak contests. Fellow Frenchman Charles 'Biboche' Delahaye played one match wearing the full dress uniform of the National Guard wielding his racket in his right hand and a musket with fixed bayonet in his left. Back in the eighteenth century, yet another Frenchman, Raymond Masson, agreed to take on all comers while jumping into a barrel between every shot. Others dispensed with the use of a racket and opted for a policeman's truncheon or soda-water bottle instead.

Nor did the French have a monopoly on eccentricity. At Brighton in 1844 Mr C. Taylor upheld English honour by taking on Mr Ricardo over five sets whilst riding on a pony specially shod with leather shoes for the occasion. Taylor lost but *Bell's Life* reported that the horse enjoyed it immensely!

'Papa' Barre died in 1873 in his seventy-first year. *The Times* described him as 'the greatest player in Europe, probably that has been or will be'.

What a pity he didn't live in the lawn tennis era which was just being born. If he had, he would surely have made his distinctive mark and figured nearer the end of *Tennis's Strangest Matches*.

THE GAME FROZEN IN TIME

WORPLE ROAD, WIMBLEDON, JULY 1877

When Major Walter Clopton Wingfield patented his revolutionary new lawn tennis game under the name 'Sphairistike' in 1874 he became the inventor of the pastime and sport that grew into what we know today simply as 'tennis'.

And when Wimbledon staged the first lawn tennis tournament three years later, it started what has since become a familiar worldwide phenomenon. Back then, though, the first Wimbledon final seemed a very odd affair indeed.

There had never been a game like it before and there has never been one like it since. The 200 people who paid a shilling each to watch the final on Thursday 19 July 1877 didn't know it but they were seeing a game frozen in time.

Viewed from their perspective, familiar as they were with Real Tennis, the game of Rackets or Wingfield's Sphairistike, nothing looked quite right. Looked at from the twenty-first century, too, the view is different but equally bizarre.

Let's face it, no matter where one stands in time, the all-British final played between Spencer W. Gore and William C. Marshall remains an all-time oddity preserved in the aspic of tennis history.

When the notice for the world's first ever official lawn tennis tournament appeared in the pages of *The Field* magazine of 9 June 1877, no one knew quite what to expect. Although its practitioners had been dabbling with a form of lawn tennis ever since 1859 or thereabouts, court layouts,

18

equipment and rules were far from standardized, but the holding of an official tournament forced the issue and the Wimbledon committee drew up a definitive code. This is what the punters got at those championships.

The court was a rectangle 78 by 27 feet, the same size as it is now, although it looked mighty odd to most of the spectators. Typical courts prior to that were 'hour-glass' or 'bow-tie' shaped, narrower at the net than at the baseline, as used in Major Wingfield's version and supported by the Marylebone Cricket Club when they drew up their rulebook in 1875.

The service line was 26 feet from the net, making the serving boxes huge by the current standard of just 21 feet. Today's big servers' aces ratio would surely have neared 100 per cent but back in 1877 no one had ever tried the over-arm service. Gore and Marshall delivered the ball round-arm from no more than shoulder height and both players kept a viciously spun under-arm serve up their long-sleeved shirt for use as necessary.

Then again, today's fast servers would have had to go down the middle because the net somewhat resembled a hammock. It was 3 feet 3 inches at the centre compared to 3 feet today, but at the posts it rose to a height which now seems ludicrous, fully 5 feet compared to the current 3 feet 6 inches.

Two serves were allowed, which the spectators found a novel innovation. Previously one had been the limit but the Wimbledon committee had seen fit to introduce a 'second life' and in the process had invented that splendid tennis institution, the double fault. Serves were delivered with one foot over the baseline and one behind, but many of the deliveries broke even those favourable rules, as Gore in particular often hit the ball when he was already well on his way to the net. Umpires generally ignored such indiscretions.

Indeed net-rushing was Gore's secret weapon. No one could pass him over what Dan Maskell could have described as 'the high part of the net' without any exaggeration. And believe it or not, no player had yet gleaned enough experience to have thought of implementing the lob. It simply wasn't used.

19

The players changed ends only after each set unless the sun or wind were particularly influential. Then the umpire, sitting on an ordinary chair placed atop a kitchen table, could ask them to change after each game. There were no rest breaks of any kind. Short sets were played at 5–all, except in the final where a two-game advantage was decreed.

Meanwhile, 'let' serves were perfectly legitimate and there were no tramlines to the court as doubles was not yet in popular vogue. Scoring was as we know it today, taken from that used in Real Tennis. This was a startling innovation for the lawn game and fans of Wingfield's version found 'this infernal system' hard to follow as they played Rackets- or Badminton-style scoring, 13 up with points only scored by the 'hand-in' server.

Add in the slightly smaller but somewhat heavier balls they used, a rather flat-ended low-tensioned racket and the quaint long-trousered garb, and there is the full recipe for lawn tennis 1877-style.

Gore, a surveyor by profession, won the match 6–1, 6–2, 6–4 in just 48 minutes to win a 12-guinea prize and lift the Silver Challenge Cup. The final was, of course, interrupted by rain.

The unique nature of this match was assured because some of the rules were immediately modified before subsequent meetings. Just as strange as the conditions of the match itself though was the reaction of the winner, who evidently had no notion of what he'd started.

In giving his opinion of the new-fangled game, Gore was scathingly dismissive. 'It is extremely doubtful,' he stated, 'that anyone who has really played well at cricket, Real Tennis or even Rackets will ever seriously give his attention to lawn tennis, for in all probability the monotony of the game would choke him off before he had time to excel in it.'

Try telling that to today's millions of followers of the game that just grew and grew.

GOOD v. EVIL

Very occasionally a quite 'ordinary' match acquires retrospective interest because of subsequent events. The 1879 All Comers' Wimbledon final, which that year decided the Championship itself, is a classic and macabre example.

The bare facts are that J. T. Hartley beat Mr 'St Leger' in straight sets 6–2, 6–4, 6–2 on Tuesday 15 July in front of 1,100 spectators at Wimbledon's old Worple Road ground. Nothing could be more straightforward.

A few curiosities attaching to this contest at the time, though, should perhaps have served as a portent that it was destined for singularity and that fully 28 years after it was concluded, it would become the most notorious first-class tennis match of all time.

Shropshire-born John Thorneycroft Hartley was a decent soul, Old Harrovian and Oxford graduate, an Anglican vicar with a living at Burniston in the North Riding of Yorkshire. Not expecting to progress too far in the tournament, he neglected to obtain cover for his Sunday service and thus endured a rather flurried route to the final, which he later recounted:

'I had to come home on Saturday, take my service on Sunday, breakfast very early on Monday, drive ten miles to a station, get to London at two, and to Wimbledon just in time to play my semi-final, rather tired by my journey and in want of a meal.'

21

He won the semi, but only thanks to a God-given break for rain after which, revived by the blessed call of 'more tea, vicar?' he 'felt much refreshed and finished off all right'.

His final opponent next day was Vere Thomas 'St Leger' Goold, who entered simply under the pseudonym of 'St Leger'. That in itself was odd but not outstandingly so. Many men of station used such 'disguises' as competition tennis was thought by some critics to be rather vulgar: 'Castor', 'Pollux', 'A. Player', 'Dagger' and even 'J. Verne' were all active on the circuit.

Goold was born in County Cork in 1853, youngest son of an Irish baronet. Just a month before Wimbledon he had won the first ever Irish Championship at Fitzwilliam Square, Dublin, so came to London with a good track record. Reverend Hartley described him as 'a cheery wild Irishman and a very pretty player' and *The Field*, in reporting the final, noted that 'his style of play is very taking and effective'. Apart from some exceptionally long rallies, or 'rests' as they were then known (the final point was 49 strokes), there was little in the final to secure its place in history. In fact the most remarkable observation in *The Field*'s account was that 'Mr Ayres' balls have again come in for a great deal of praise'. Good for him.

Goold never appeared at Wimbledon again and it was not until 1907, when he was 54 and Hartley had attained the celestial heights of Honorary Canon of Ripon, that the shocking postscript was written.

After his marriage to French-born Marie Girodin in Bayswater, London, in 1891, it seems Goold fell on relatively hard times; he and his thrice-married bride, who admirably adds to the mystique of the tale by appearing on the marriage certificate as Violet Wilkinson, lived on their wits, moving first to Montreal, then opening a laundry in Waterloo, near Liverpool, in 1903, before opting for something of a contrast by settling in Monte Carlo.

There they desperately plied the gaming tables and made the acquaintance of a wealthy Danish widow, Emma Liven, from whom they secured 'loans' in good faith.

On the morning of Tuesday 6 August 1907 the Goolds took

the 5.38 am train from Monte Carlo to Marseilles, where they alighted and deposited a trunk and large handbag with instructions for them to be forwarded to London. A porter perturbed by a smell coming from the luggage called in the police and the dismembered body of Emma Liven was found neatly packed inside. Goold's chop shot had proved effective for the last time.

The trial in Monte Carlo in December lasted three days. There were spurious explanations galore before Goold admitted to the murder which had taken place in his flat in the Villa Menesini on 4 August. Mrs Liven had, it transpired, had the temerity to ask for the return of a 'loan'. Mrs Goold, meanwhile, had proved a willing accomplice.

Despite appeals, St Leger was sentenced to penal servitude for life on Devil's Island in French Guiana. Mrs Goold, rather harshly, was first sentenced to death but this was later reduced to life imprisonment in Montpellier, where she died in 1914. St Leger lasted only until 8 September 1909. Canon Hartley, meanwhile, lived an extremely pleasant life and passed away in Knaresborough, Yorkshire, in 1935, aged 86.

'St Leger' Goold remains the only convicted murderer ever to have contested a Wimbledon final; homicidal maniacs, not having sufficient time to practice, generally fall in the early rounds. The 1879 final takes its place in the record books as the match between the vicar and the murderer, when 'Good' took on 'Evil' and prevailed without dropping a set.

ONE SHOT AFTER ANOTHER

BEDFORD, JULY 1883

The vicarage lawn seems synonymous with the early days of lawn tennis, for many a gentle social game was played on just such a greensward.

The link between affairs of the heart and the playing of tennis in Victorian society is also a strong one. What better way for a diffident young gentleman and a demure young lady to meet in circumstances sufficiently informal for social barriers to be eroded, yet respectable enough for a sense of propriety to be maintained? In mixed pairs, after all, one kept to one's own side, and in a mixed singles the net assumed an almost chaperonal character, dividing the parties at all times even when cheeks became flushed or ardour threatened to wax.

Enough clothes were worn, too, to prevent provocative glimpses of flesh. Dull it may sound, but potentially sensuous enough for love to often find a way. The term 'courtship' proved an apt one indeed.

It is an idyllic image but once in a while illusions must be shattered, none more horribly so than in the game that took place in the evening of Tuesday 17 July 1883 which ended in grisly murder and suicide.

A young gent named Hubert Wigram Vesey Vere had passed from Bedford Grammar School into the army and was posted for foreign service. Prior to leaving for Egypt he made the acquaintance of a respectable young lady, Eleanor Eveleen

McKay, recently moved to Bedford with her widowed mother. Vere, it later transpired, had been somewhat smitten by Eleanor's charms but, displaying typical Victorian reserve, had failed utterly to declare his feelings.

Quite possibly pining, and deciding army life just wasn't for him, he sold his commission and returned from his exotic posting in Tel-el-Kebir to the stolid familiarity of Bedford and the comfort of his mother's home. Feeling sure Eleanor would be 'waiting' he planned some serious wooing.

But alas, a young Bedford solicitor had already presented his own case with sufficient vigour for Eleanor and him to be a regular item on the tennis court and Hubert Vere's declarations were rebuffed. Suffice it to say the boy Bertie was no longer in the frame or, as *The Times* so succinctly put it in their report, 'Miss McKay did not reciprocate his attachment.'

It was a pleasant summer evening for a game of lawn tennis as Miss McKay and her new partner played the son and daughter of the rector of St Cuthbert's on the vicarage lawn. There has never been a 'what happened next?' quite like it.

The columns of *The Times* gave the facts the following day: 'It was 7.30 in the evening when Vere entered the tennis enclosure and walking straight up to Miss McKay he drew a revolver from his pocket and shot her in the region of the heart. While attention was directed to her he placed the gun to his head and shot himself.'

The blood ran freely as the evening shadows lengthened. When help arrived, a third chamber of the brand new six-chambered weapon was also found to be loaded. Vere's rival, it seems, may have been lucky to escape unscathed.

At the inquest a verdict of wilful murder was returned. Rosella Darlow, a servant at the local inn, delivered the following evidence: 'He came in seeming to be in an excited state and bought eight pennyworth of brandy. He tendered a florin for it but dashed away without taking the change. A few minutes later I took it to him on the tennis lawn but found him dead and the lady unconscious. Within a few minutes she died too.'

Other witnesses spoke of a remote reserve and strangeness

that had marked Vere's manner since his return from Egypt. A verdict of 'suicide during temporary insanity' was returned. A letter addressed to his mother was found on Vere's body but its contents were never revealed.

The undisputed winner of the most macabre game in tennis history was the unstoppable 'green-eyed monster'. Jealousy had consumed Hubert Vere, the red mist descended, and the classic crime of passion was perpetrated.

On a vicarage lawn in Bedford the two deadliest shots in tennis history had left their gruesome mark.

THE GOVERNMENT v. THE OPPOSITION

PRINCE'S GROUND, LONDON, JULY 1883

It is surely the supreme way to settle political differences. Just imagine Tony Blair (Labour, seeded 1) taking on William Hague (Conservative, seeded 2) on the tennis court. The Speaker of the House of Commons would undoubtedly keep order from the umpire's chair and it would be as entertaining a contest as even the best of Prime Minister's Question Times. Who knows? But we won't hold our breath. Yet on 31 July 1883 a match of this sort did take place when the government faced the opposition in a doubles challenge. The two teams carried the sensibilities of the populace, for politically Britain was a divided nation. As Guardsman Willis so admirably pointed out in Gilbert and Sullivan's *Iolanthe* just a year earlier:

Every boy and every gal,
That's born into the world alive,
Is either a little Liberal,
Or else a little Conservative.

Quite. Whether Queen Victoria was amused at some of her leading statesmen scurrying about a tennis court has not been recorded, but perhaps the absence of Prime Minister William Ewart Gladstone himself from the Liberal government's team of four suggests that a line had been judiciously drawn in the

27

interests of avoiding a complete circus. Then again, he was 73 at the time.

Instead it was his 29-year-old youngest son Herbert Gladstone, Liberal MP for Leeds and a mere junior lord of the treasury, who led the government team and spun rackets with the opposition at the courts attached to The Prince's Club (now Hans Place) in Belgravia, an establishment well suited to players of such celebrity.

Established in 1854 as a centre for Real Tennis and Rackets, it later embraced the lawn game and included a cricket ground and roller-skating rink among its lavish facilities, with Turkish baths, refreshment rooms, bar, viewing gallery and gardens by Capability Brown. And today's tennis players thought *they* discovered the Health and Leisure Club concept!

Starring for the Conservative opposition was Arthur Balfour, who had played in one of the earliest of all experimental lawn tennis games back in 1869, so there was some rare talent on display. Rare political talent, too, for A. J. Balfour would himself become prime minister in 1902. Even then, he always found time for tennis and was a regular Wimbledon visitor.

This was no lightly taken contest. Twice postponed through bad weather, they might easily have called it off but finally faced each other on a pleasant Tuesday afternoon in July. *The Times* furnished the results:

Match 1: Lord George Hamilton & The Hon. S. Herbert (Opposition) beat H. Brand & R. T. Reid (Government) 6–4, 6–2.

Match 2: H. Gladstone & A. Grey (Government) beat Sir W. Hart-Dyke & A. J. Balfour (Opposition) 6–4, 2–6, 6–2.

Match 3: Sir W. Hart-Dyke & A. J. Balfour (Opposition) beat H. Brand & R. T. Reid (Government) 6–5, 6–2.

Match 4: H. Gladstone & A. Grey (Government) beat Lord George Hamilton & The Hon. S. Herbert (Opposition) 6–3, 6–4.

Keen to avoid any accusations of partisanship *The Times* confined their report to a simple and surely uncontroversial statement: 'Thus honours were divided, the result being two matches each.'

But wait a minute. The Conservatives won 5 sets to the Liberals' 4, a total of 43 games to 39. A double victory for the opposition.

'But surely my honourable friend will concede,' replies the government, 'that Gladstone and Grey were the only unbeaten pairing. On that alone we must prevail.' The government takes the honours!

Nothing but conjectural spin-doctoring of course. Anything that was said was strictly confined to the privacy of the bar. Even in lawn tennis it seems there is no way around the perpetual impasse of political stalemate.

THE 'STRONG' v. THE 'FAIR'

EXMOUTH, AUGUST 1888

Let's get this straight from the start. Men and women were not only different sexes in Victorian England, but perceived by sections of polite society as entirely different species.

The 'fair sex', rather quaintly referred to by men simply as 'the fair', could not possibly expect to compete with 'the strong', and their participation in lawn tennis was viewed by the men with a sense of amused amazement.

Even as late as 1903, when the ladies' game was well established, a leading writer pontificated: 'Most ladies believe that a ball struck horizontally over a net will bound off the ground vertically as if it has been dropped straight from the skies.'

Another earlier work suggested that 'the ladies will surely have some difficulty in understanding the scoring'.

There is one small flaw in all this Victorian sexism. The ladies who did play tennis treated this male chauvinism with exactly the contempt it deserved. Beneath the long skirts and restricting stays were athletic bodies and healthy hearts. They played with gusto, and many played exceptionally well.

As debate raged, the first high profile Battle of the Sexes match was inevitable. Representing 'the strong', Mr Ernest Renshaw, aged 27. And for 'the fair', Miss Lottie Dod, aged 17.

Dateline Monday 13 August 1888. Venue, Exmouth in Devon, England.

30

Leamington-born Renshaw was the less-talented twin brother of the phenomenal Willie, who won the Wimbledon singles title seven times in the 1880s. Ernest nabbed it just once, but as that was in 1888 it earned him the right to face that year's ladies champion.

Cheshire-born Lottie, known as the 'Little Wonder', had won the 1887 Wimbledon title at her first attempt. She was just 15 years and 285 days old, which remains a singles record to this day. She won it again in 1888 and in fact was never beaten at Wimbledon.

Despite Lottie's record, a level start against Ernest was felt completely out of the question and she was given a 30–love lead in every game.

A substantial crowd each paid one shilling to enter the Exmouth Ground, proceeds going to the local dispensary. They certainly got their money's worth.

Young Charlotte stormed to a 4–0 lead in the opening set, actually scoring more points than Ernest. *Pastime* magazine reported that 'Renshaw then perceived that he had no ordinary lady opponent, and from that moment every stroke was keenly contested, both players doing their utmost to gain the victory.'

Lottie took the first set 6–2 and, as Renshaw fretted, the crowd wondered whether a handicap was necessary at all.

Renshaw led 5–3 in the second but Miss Dod 'played most pluckily' to level at 5–all before going down 7–5. So to the decider, which Renshaw again nicked 7–5. The statistics showed each player winning 16 games, with 95 points to Renshaw and 52 to Dod.

The report summed up as follows: 'Miss Dod surprised the spectators by the brilliancy of her play, several times going to the net to score by volleys. She played so well that Renshaw had to run about as much as against a first-rate player of his own sex. The lady could not, of course, stand the strain so well as her opponent, and palpably tired towards the end.'

Despite the barbed ending to the report, the conclusion was unavoidable. This was a moral victory for the ladies!

There is no doubt that Lottie Dod was the Martina Hingis of her day. She won five Wimbledon titles but some years elected not to enter due to a lack of serious opposition; in 1889 she spent Wimbledon fortnight on a walking holiday in Scotland. And lest any man should still be scoffing, there is more. Lottie was captain of England's ladies' hockey team, Women's Open Golf Champion in 1904, the best lady archer in England, an accomplished figure skater, fine choral singer, expert bridge player, keen cricketer and the first lady to go down the Cresta Run. Truly the first female sporting 'superstar'.

She died in Sway, Hampshire, on 27 June 1960 during Wimbledon fortnight, aged 88. Her long-forgotten game in Exmouth 72 years earlier gave women's tennis the boost it needed. And the 'Little Wonder' certainly gave the men something to wonder about.

OH, DO LET'S WATCH CHIPP!

TEIGNMOUTH, AUGUST 1888

It didn't matter where Herbert Chipp played, the story was always the same. Who could have blamed him for becoming paranoid? Yet in fact he maintained a dignity and geniality that all who got to know him truly admired. And that despite being subject to a whispering campaign that followed him wherever he took his racket – home or abroad, there was simply no escape.

'He's got no backhand' was what they always said. That is, as anyone who has struggled with that particular stroke knows only too well, the sort of below-the-belt snide tennis insult that implies a level of inbuilt feebleness to be utterly ashamed of. They might just as well have unfurled courtside banners with foot-high letters screaming HERBERT CHIPP WETS HIS PANTS.

Even those who hadn't seen him play were quick to accept the assertions of those who had and were equally quick to spread the apparently scurrilous jibe: 'You ought to see Chipp play. They say he's got no backhand' was on everybody's lips. Quite simply it became the talk of Victorian tennis society: whatever court he was on, even in a far-flung corner of the grounds, people would seek him out to check on the evidence and to a man and woman they always agreed. Our 'Bert' was certainly a little light in the backhand department.

Even when he played well the jungle drums wouldn't stop. Take the annual tournament in Teignmouth, Devon, in 1888.

In the singles final on Saturday 25 August, he annihilated the Midland Counties Champion, J. R. Daykin, 6–0, 6–1, 6–0 in fine style yet still the tennis fans said the same. For good measure he also won the doubles, so it wasn't as if he was a bad player, nor was Teignmouth a one-off. His record would show that he took many fine scalps in his day and reached the Wimbledon semi-finals, no less, in 1884.

Not only that. Here was a man of such standing in society that he was elected the first ever secretary of the British Lawn Tennis Association and was a leading light on the International Selection Committee.

The whole thing would have been shameful but for the fact that it was absolutely true. The fact is that every single game Herbert Chipp played in was an oddity and the 'no backhand' jibe was nothing of the sort. It was, instead, a compliment that expressed extreme admiration for Chipp's game for, in a Victorian society much taken with novelty, he was a veritable curiosity, a marvel no less. 'Upon my word,' they cried, 'he's ambidextrous!'

Therein is the plain truth behind Chipp's much talked about game. He was the first high-profile player to solve the backhand problem by swapping his racket from one hand to another to play every shot as a forehand.

That very rare skill is something few have ever mastered in over a century of tennis history. (The now popular double-hander, perfected by many, is a different and easier thing altogether.)

The Italian Georgio de Stefani was another ambidextrous artist, good enough to beat most leading players in the 1930s but perhaps most 'celebrated' for blowing a staggering 18 match points in his Davis Cup match against America's Wilmer Allison in 1930.

The ladies, too, have had their practitioners – the American Beverley Fleitz was runner-up in the 1955 Wimbledon singles playing a totally ambidextrous game.

There was, though, only one Herbert Chipp, 'king of the ambies'. His epitaph writes itself: 'He's got no backhand.'

CHAMPION CHOKER

WORPLE ROAD, WIMBLEDON, JULY 1889

As things stood prior to Wimbledon 2001, American Pete Sampras had done it seven times. Sweden's Bjorn Borg did it a mere five times. But it is a British man who still holds the joint record with 'Pistol Pete' as we go to press for the most Wimbledon men's singles championships: William Charles Renshaw was champion an astonishing seven times back in the 1880s.

It is true that on five of these occasions 'Willie' only had to win one match because right until 1921 the title holder 'stood out' until the winner of the All Comers' final came through to face him in the 'Challenge Round'. But such was Renshaw's dominance one suspects he might have done it anyway.

What is certain, though, is that he wouldn't have clinched his record-breaking seventh win in 1889 but for the alarming propensity for 'choking' displayed by his British rival Harry Sibthorpe Barlow. Although the term wasn't used back then, the ability to clutch defeat from the jaws of victory is as old as the game itself and Barlow, arguably, was its first champion exponent.

With six titles already in the bag, Willie had lost out in 1888 although, by way of keeping it in the family, his twin brother Ernest had taken the championship instead. That meant Willie had to do things the hard way in 1889, going into the hat with the rest to endure the hurly-burly of the All Comers' draw.

Willie's progress to the All Comers' final was relatively

35

untroubled. There, on Saturday 6 July, Barlow, who had never been that far before, awaited him.

The 29-year-old Barlow, a Middlesex county cricketer, started sensationally and took the first set 6–3. When he held his nerve to take the second 7–5, a major shock loomed. Twice in the third he was just two points away from wrapping it up in straight sets but Renshaw hung in to take it 8–6. More of a hiccup than a choke for Barlow, though, for he still had the upper hand.

The effort of taking the third set appeared to have shattered Renshaw. He looked spent and at 5–2 down in the fourth, the game seemed all but up. But according to the report in *The Field* he suddenly began to play 'like a cat, running and scraping to stay in the match'.

Six times in all Barlow reached match point. Six times he blew it. And none more dramatically than in the fourteenth game. Trailing 6–7 and 30–40 Renshaw approached the match point against him aggressively, charging the net behind his serve. But in his eagerness to get there he overpushed himself and as the serve sailed in he fell headlong and dropped his racket.

Any moderate drive from Barlow would have won the match but torn between keeping cool, making sure and perhaps a quixotic desire to be seen as sporting, he threw up a patty half-lob.

The reports tell us that Renshaw, down but not out, 'picked up his racket, dashed back in pursuit of the ball, caught up with it, and won the exchange'. Having choked big time, Barlow lost the set 10–8.

But if Renshaw thought that was as good as 'it', he was sadly mistaken. Barlow put the choke behind him to go all out for a famous win. As phenomenal tennis took him to 5–0, a betting man in the stands offered 100–1 against Renshaw coming back. A Renshaw fan countered with the defiant reply, 'You don't know Willie.'

Sure enough Barlow choked yet again and the six-time champ came back to 5–5. Barlow went ahead 6–5. Then Renshaw took the last three games to close the match 8–6.

After a contest, which remains one of the most astonishing in tennis history, Willie duly beat his brother in the Challenge Round two days later to take his seventh title.

Harry Barlow never did win Wimbledon but his place as the choker par excellence remained secure until he achieved yet another remarkable feat in 1891.

THE WRONG-SHAPED COURT

RICHMOND, JUNE 1890

When the first ever Richmond Lawn Tennis Tournament was held at the Athletic Association Grounds in the Deer Park in June 1890, no one noticed anything unusual. It might have been their first major event but tennis had been around for long enough then for everyone to know the ropes. Or should we say 'nearly' everyone.

The tournament organizers felt most honoured that esteemed guests had agreed to attend the finals to present the prizes. The Duke and Duchess of Teck were said to be keen followers of the game and their stately White House residence boasted a number of its own courts.

They arrived with due pomp and ceremony in a rather grand carriage. Their daughter Princess Victoria, later to be Queen Mary, accompanied them. Onlookers might have questioned how keen they really were when the party opted not to step out of the carriage to see the action in the men's doubles in which W. and H. Baddeley, the famous twins, faced A. W. 'Baby' Gore and F. Haskett-Smith.

The solution, though, was simple enough as the coachman coaxed his horses into pole courtside position for a grandstand view even better than the royal box.

Tournament referee Nicholas Lane Jackson, too, began to wonder what grasp the VIP party had of the vagaries of the game when the duchess asked him if the fellows were professionals. 'There are no professionals in tennis, ma'am,' he explained.

Having already betrayed a somewhat hazy knowledge of proceedings it might have been wise for these early prototypes of the classic corporate guest to have kept quiet but the duchess decided to go for the hat trick.

'Excuse me, Mr Jackson,' she said, calling the unfailingly polite and admirably tolerant official over to her carriage, 'I have another question.'

Even Jackson spluttered into his moustache at this one: 'Why is the court a rectangle?' spake the aristocratic personage.

Jackson might have been forgiven for wondering if it was a fiendish riddle but there was no punch line to this one. The White House courts, it transpired, were still marked out in the hour-glass shape abandoned by lawn tennis fully 13 years earlier: in 1877 the first Wimbledon Championships' committee decided that straight lines looked much neater and would protect linesmen from being driven round the bend.

The referee's discreet explanation was greeted by the duchess with genuine astonishment: 'Mr Jackson says our courts are obsolete!' she chided the duke, whose own happy inhabitation of a blissfully anachronistic world had just been irrevocably shattered.

Next day, meanwhile, the courts at the ducal pile were promptly marked up and ceremoniously passed correct by the all-knowing Jackson for which he was treated to a rather grand Sunday lunch.

Just like the high court judge who once asked 'Who is Gazza?' and our current queen who stunned quiz show icon Richard Whiteley with 'What is *Countdown*?' the Duchess of Teck proved that being out of touch is a timeless art and that strangeness is sometimes purely in the eye of the beholder.

BARLOW'S DOUBLE DATE

CHELTENHAM, JUNE 1891

One fine midsummer day in the long-forgotten June of 1891, Harry Sibthorpe Barlow achieved a feat which would warm the cockles of any self-respecting quizmaster, especially one bent on devious interrogation: 'And the next question is "True or False?" – the winner of the Cheltenham Open Tennis Tournament of 1891 was H. S. Barlow.'

The answer is that it's 'true' for Barlow, known hitherto as the Champion Choker, did win the Cheltenham Open that year. But it's also 'false' as he lost it as well.

Confused? So were the shameful goings-on in genteel and leafy Cheltenham.

This is a tale of three courts which starts at Queen's Bench Court No. 5 in London on the afternoon of Tuesday 21 April 1891. There were many tennis players and officials present, no balls were hit, but there were verbal volleys aplenty in this classic lawn tennis lawsuit which reached match point two days later on the Thursday lunchtime.

Edited highlights of the contest must here suffice. May we present the antagonists, Webb and another *v.* Taylor and others. Your referee will be Mr Justice Hawkins.

Webb Brothers, the plaintiffs, were lessees of the Montpellier Gardens in Cheltenham. In February 1890 they had entered into an agreement with the defendants, Captain Taylor, General Houghton and Mr E. C. Studd. These stout fellows three were the committee of the annual Cheltenham

Lawn Tennis Tournament, hitherto held on the East Gloucestershire Cricket Ground. The agreement was that the 1890 tournament would be held at the splendidly commodious Montpellier Gardens, rather a coup for the Brothers Webb as their venture into the leisure industry thus far had been rather more industry on their part than the leisure they had hoped to enjoy from the profits, which were disappointingly down.

The deal was seemingly straightforward, and I quote verbatim: 'Webb Brothers shall provide courts in good order and condition together with tents and other necessary equipment for the annual lawn tennis tournament on 10 June and shall pay the sum of £120 to the Tournament Committee in consideration of which Messrs Webb shall be entitled to receive all gate-money together with certain other privileges.'

Viewed from a distance, any competent business guru might spot the risk at a stroke. The tennis committee had no outlay and no risk. The pleasure garden owners had to invest on ground preparation up front and pay the £120 concession before even getting a sniff of the coveted crinkly stuff.

But this was the big one and they pulled all the stops out to make it work. The Webb Brothers smelt money. The Gardens were taking off. A Whitsuntide fête and a military tournament had attracted vast crowds. The tennis, surely, would be a success.

Enter one harassed groundsman, surveying the courts on which the military bands had marched and the crowds frolicked. Enter too the committee triumvirate.

On 1 June, nine days before the tournament was to start, the secretary Captain Taylor sent a letter to Webbs saying that he considered the courts 'could not be got ready in acceptable condition' and that the tournament would be switched to the cricket ground. The plug had been well and truly pulled with the Webbs having already spent over £100 on preparation.

The 1890 tournament duly took place at the cricket ground and the Webbs sued the tournament committee for damages and loss of profits.

In legal terms it was a corker. The central question was, 'Were the courts in good order?' 'No,' screamed the

41

defendants, wheeling in a host of witnesses to back them up. Dash it all, there were 'bare patches' don't you know. A Colonel Bainbridge had seen men 'dibbling' on court. He had to explain to a packed courtroom variously confused and shocked (one lady juror surely blushed) that this was a process adopted out in India whereby small tufts of grass were implanted on a bare patch to make it look green. Turf doctors were called as expert witnesses and declared that some of the courts 'wouldn't have lasted for half a day'.

The Webbs countered with equally crisp shots of their own, calling on leading players and experienced tournament referees who had tested or viewed the courts and pronounced them 'entirely satisfactory'.

As in any closely contested match, both sides felt they deserved to take it. In the event, after a long summing up, the jury retired for just 15 minutes and found in favour of the tournament committee. The Webb Brothers were up the creek without a paddle. 'Fix,' cried some. 'Old Boys' act,' accused others.

And so to 1891. Understandably, the committee again opted to hold the tournament at the cricket ground but, such was the strength of feeling among many of the players and officials, who felt the Webb Brothers had been shabbily treated, that they decided to organize a rival tournament at the same time in Montpellier Gardens, this one under the auspices of the Gloucestershire County Lawn Tennis Club. Both called themselves the Cheltenham Open, so honour was satisfied and the charming Gloucestershire spa town, in which George III had taken the waters a hundred years before, became a split camp in which reputations were put at stake and where bitter rivalries prevailed. June 1891 was an interesting month in tennis circles.

So to the dénouement in this tale of three courts. The other two, blessedly, were of the green variety on which the finals were played. Entirely unfazed by all the shenanigans, many of the players entered both tournaments, giving the referees Bonham Carter Evelegh and Nicholas Lane Jackson the hardest job of all. As the temperatures bubbled up, meteorologically and metaphorically, so did their blood pressures, but these two cool-headed fellows, both big names in Victorian sport, reached the finals bang on time thanks to some shoehorn and sliderule scheduling.

Which is where Barlow comes in. He reached the final of the men's open singles at both venues. On finals day he lost to Ernest Lewis at Montpellier in straight sets 6–4, 6–3, 6–2. It is not recorded whether he blamed the state of the courts.

Undeterred, he hot-footed it straight over to the cricket ground to take on T. D. Cummins. Perhaps Barlow felt at home there as he was a fine county cricketer with Middlesex; he won the title in straight sets 7–5, 6–3, 6–2.

Barlow had achieved the apparently impossible feat of being both the winning and losing finalist in the Cheltenham Open Tennis Tournament on the same day.

There ends the tale. When all the dust had settled, the lawn tennis journal *Pastime* summed it up with admirable circumspection, befitting the true gentility of Cheltenham, as 'this most unfortunate squabble'.

LUCK OF THE IRISH

OLYMPIC GAMES, ATHENS, APRIL 1896

When the ancient Olympic Games were revived in 1896 as what we now know as the first of the legendary series of Modern Olympics, lawn tennis was included as one of the events and described by the official report as 'this most charming athletic game'.

Despite being still two years short of its twenty-first birthday in terms of tournament competition, the charm and popularity of that delightful youngster tennis was indeed already firmly established and played extensively on the Continent.

Therein lay a problem, because all the leading players had so taken to the comforting routine and annual ritual of the flourishing tennis circuit that they were by and large inclined not to step off that enjoyable merry-go-round to undertake an arduous journey to Greece to play in a tournament neither tried nor tested. Result, a shortage of willing competitors.

They say that sometimes out of adversity emerges triumph. They might also say, although no one ever has, that out of this particular adversity emerged a 26-year-old Irishman keen to get himself fixed up with a holiday and willing to go with the flow to get himself a half-decent suntan. When in Rome, do as the Romans do. A lesser known but far more entertaining axiom is 'When in Athens, do as the Irish do.'

That might well have been the motto of John Boland. Any red-blooded male able to have survived his school years unscathed, having been blessed with the second Christian name of Mary, must surely have a touch of spirit about him and John Mary Pius Boland drew on that very spirit to secure himself a place in tennis and Olympic history which has eccentricity written all over it.

Born in Dublin, Ireland, on 16 September 1870, John Boland benefited from a broad education that taught him to have a bash at things. After attending the Catholic University School in Dublin he transferred to the Edgbaston Oratory and thence on to Christ's College, Oxford, headed for a career in the Law.

In 1894, Boland invited a Greek acquaintance, Thrasyvoalos Manaos (who, in the interests of the proof-readers' union, will be referred to subsequently as 'his Greek friend') to speak at the Oxford Union. This Greek friend chose as his subject 'The Revival of the Modern Olympic Games' and he and Boland hit it off to such a degree that they subsequently kept in touch and became close friends.

When Boland was invited by his Greek friend to spend the Easter holidays of 1896 in Athens he packed his bags eagerly, no doubt carrying thoughts of ancient history, a spot of sunshine and a jolly good time with him on his journey.

Although he liked a game of tennis, he certainly arrived in Athens with no intention of entering the Olympic tournament.

It so happened, though, that his genial Greek host was a member of the organizing committee charged with making a success of the men's singles and doubles events, which had been firmly posted into the itinerary. A projected entry of twelve, although a manageable round number, was hardly an impressive field, and Boland was persuaded to swell the ranks to an interesting thirteen from four nations.

Boland had dabbled in tournament play a little in England, but he had no real form to speak of and no experience of international competition. It is said that when he was asked to enter he was at first most reluctant. To be sure, he fancied a game of tennis; he was after all on his holidays, but 'No thank you, not in the Olympic competition.'

'But you will not find another court anywhere in Athens,'

45

asserted the Greek friend, bending the truth as only Olympic Committee members can. 'In that case, I shall play,' said Boland. When it came to a rush of blood to the head, the Irishman's corpuscles positively sprinted and the cranium that fate-laden day was displaying the Vacancies sign.

Thus it was that an Irish law student on holiday came to win his way through to the first ever Olympic lawn tennis final. The forehand drive held up remarkably well; the serve did its stuff to order; even the backhand was on song. It goes without saying that 26-year-old John Mary Pius Boland won the singles final to take gold, beating the Greek hope Dionisios Kasdaglis in straight sets, 7–5, 6–4, 6–1.

Being a friendly soul, the genial Irishman mixed freely with his fellow competitors. Such a shame it was for Fritz Traun, a German entrant, that his doubles partner had withdrawn because of injury. Boland sympathized heartily. Might it not be possible, mused the organizing committee, by this time desperate to give out medals to anyone on the Greek mainland who owned a tennis racket, for the genial Irishman to play, as it were, as a German?

Boland let slip that, after having left Oxford, he had continued his studies at Bonn University. Moreover, while in Athens he planned to spend some time with a friend, Heinrich Schliemann, the famous German archaeologist. Then that settled it, he was half German!

Boland said *Ja* and again it goes without saying that 'Germany' took the gold medal in the men's doubles. Again the poor Greeks had to content themselves with silver, Boland and Traun beating the hapless Kasdaglis and his partner Petrokokkinos 6–2, 6–4 in the best of three sets final.

Where does a double gold medal winner go from there? A year later Boland was called to the Bar; not to continue celebrating his unlikely triumph, but to pursue a career in Law. Never one to be able to say no, he also served as Member of Parliament for South Kerry from 1900 to 1918, was general secretary of the Catholic Truth Society for 21 years and a member of the commission for the foundation of the National University of Ireland.

Where on earth did he find time to pursue his burgeoning tennis career? The answer is, he didn't. Boland's name figured no more in the game's history. But it will remain in the record books for ever as the winner of the two lawn tennis gold medals at the inaugural Modern Olympics.

With a sense of timing equally as fortuitous as his choice of holiday dates, Boland died in Westminster, London, aged 77, on 17 March 1958, St Patrick's Day.

SEEING DOUBLES

DUBLIN, IRELAND, JUNE 1896

'Claiming a larger attendance than even Wimbledon, and infinitely more sociable, the Irish Championship meeting in Fitzwilliam Square, Dublin, was the most popular meeting of the year. The players were made honorary members of the Fitzwilliam Club and were entertained lavishly at innumerable pleasant functions.'

Thus wrote the editor of *The Field* magazine in praise of the fair city's annual lawn tennis extravaganza.

Spectators attending the final of the gentlemen's doubles competition in 1896 might well have thought that the effects of enthusiastic revelry had finally impaired their eyesight.

In fact they weren't seeing double but they were certainly seeing 'doubles', for crusing their way to victory over R. F. Doherty and H. A. Nisbet were the British identical twins Wilfred and Herbert Baddeley.

Born on 11 January 1872 in Bromley, Kent, the remarkable lookalikes took the Irish title 6–3, 7–5, 6–0 as routinely as they had won other doubles events wherever they travelled. Four times they nabbed the Wimbledon Championships together.

Yet even odder still than the unusual coincidence of identical twins becoming the world's leading tennis pairing was that they weren't the first. Fellow clones Willie and Ernest Renshaw swept all before them before the Baddeleys took their crown, winning Oxford twice, Dublin four times and Wimbledon five.

Maybe there was some spooky genetic experimentation going on in the world of Victorian tennis because it didn't end there. The Allen twins, 'C. G.' and 'E. R.', were a double act on the circuit in more ways than one, perfecting such amusing antics and patter that crowds gravitated to their courts just for the entertainment. While the Baddeleys did the business in the Emerald Isle, the Allens cleaned up at the 1896 Scottish championships.

The tennis world must have wondered if this familial plotting wasn't getting rather out of hand as the fraternal couplings were accompanied by a number of sister acts. The first Wimbledon ladies' singles in 1884 was won by Maud Watson when she beat her older sister Lilian in the final. Meanwhile, the Misses Steedman bagged the All England ladies' doubles championships in 1889 and superstar Lottie Dod helped herself to the All England mixed title three years later, naturally enough, with her brother.

Nor did the epidemic confine itself to British shores. American brothers C. B. and S. R. Neel won the US doubles in 1896 while sisters from the famous Roosevelt family celebrated 1890 with their US ladies' doubles win. Seven years later the Atkinson girls took the same crown. Europe, too, held its end up as the French Vacherot brothers took their national title, and all before Queen Victoria had vacated the British throne.

The trend, of course, has continued. Amritraj, Gullikson, Mayer, Lloyd, Austin, Jordan, Gerulaitis, McEnroe and many more are all well-known names in sibling tennis. Venus and Serena Williams, too, are said to be quite useful!

But nothing can compare with the late nineteenth century. Every remarkable sequence must come to an end though, and when the Baddeley twins lost their Wimbledon doubles crown in 1897 they never regained it.

The pair that beat them made sure of that by winning it a cool eight times in nine years. In the distinctly spooky fraternal spirit of the times, they were Reggie and Laurie Doherty, the most celebrated brothers in tennis history.

A HEATED ENCOUNTER

QUEEN'S CLUB, LONDON, JULY 1900

A century ago, the London Open Championships at Queen's Club generally followed Wimbledon, giving the players a chance to variously unwind or settle old scores as was their wont. But when England's Miss Dorothea Douglass played the American champion Miss Marion Jones in the second round of the handicap singles in 1900, both players got rather more than they bargained for.

Ealing-born Dorothea, daughter of a parson, came to Queen's that year as defeated Wimbledon quarter-finalist, but with immense promise. She was to take the Wimbledon ladies' singles title a remarkable seven times between 1903 and 1913 and, under her married name of Mrs Lambert-Chambers, did more than any player of her time to advance the cause of British ladies' tennis. For good measure, she was All England badminton champion in 1903 and 1904 and later became a professional hockey player. This girl had guts.

So too had Marion Jones, reigning as United States National Champion. She had stamina too. In 1898, when the women's singles in the USA were played over five sets, she lost narrowly in the final to Juliette Atkinson over a marathon 51 games. She, too, came straight from a quarter-final defeat at Wimbledon.

The weather in London in July, as many tennis fans will know to their cost, can be wet, but as Misses Douglass and Jones took to the court on this particular day the press reported the match being played 'under a fiercely hot sun, with scarcely a breath of air available'.

With that in mind, the matter of ladies' attire becomes one of significance. From the earliest days of lawn tennis, ladies had adopted the only garb considered decent, effectively the same costume as they would have worn at a summer garden party.

This meant an elaborately flounced, ground-length dress with high neck and tight waist, worn with a large hat, and underneath it all a steel-boned corset, bustle, several petticoats and long drawers.

It was, of course, the most ludicrous costume for tennis, and the ladies knew it, but in an age when it was considered unseemly for a true lady to be seen to perspire in public, let alone show much bare flesh, that was the norm. Incidentally, the reason tennis wear is traditionally white is that it was the only colour not to obviously betray those beastly perspiration marks.

By 1900 such strictures had lapsed slightly and both bustles and hats were optional, but when Dorothea and Marion commenced battle on this particular 'Phew what a scorcher!' day, they were, to put it bluntly, wearing far too many clothes.

At least, that is, in all respects but one. Being spirited women keen to divest themselves of anything that decency would permit, they opted to give the hats a miss on the very day when common sense, rather than a sense of liberation, ought to have prevailed.

'Hatless, the pair fought doggedly for over two and a half hours,' said the reports, 'until Miss Douglass eventually triumphed 10–8, 2–6, 7–5 after being 5–1 down in the final set.' Of perspiration there must have been much. And that means dehydration, especially in an era when rests and drinks between games were strangely not even contemplated.

Marion Jones was 'taken to the dressing room in a fainting condition'; Dorothea Douglass 'had an attack of sunstroke upon reaching home'. It was still to be another 19 years before the legendary French player Suzanne Lenglen would, finally, as one player put it, 'deliver the women from the tyranny of corsets' and change the face of the game for ever.

In the meantime, the ladies simply blamed the men and all the hypocrisy that their double standards of behaviour implied. Emancipation, both political and on the tennis court, would have to wait awhile but at Queen's that day the wilting pair might have taken some devilish comfort from the final postscript to this hottest of contests.

The male umpire also suffered an attack of sunstroke and was reported to have 'been ill for some time'.

It was the only match in history with three 'strokes' too many but one which surely finished 'Advantage ladies'. At least they'd played the game.

MURIEL'S ACTION REPLAY

WORPLE ROAD, WIMBLEDON, JULY 1902

Newcastle-born Muriel Robb only won Wimbledon once and she was certainly made to do it the hard way. What happened in her Challenge Round final against hot favourite Charlotte Sterry has never been repeated in Wimbledon history. But it was a 'repeat' itself that secured the match its place in the tennis annals.

Charlotte Sterry, the former 'Chattie' Cooper, had made winning Wimbledon something of a habit. Four times since 1895 she'd taken the ladies' singles and had been runner-up on three occasions, appearing in the Challenge Final seven times in a row. At 31, she was nearing the veteran stage but fully expected to win again. A contemporary tribute said it all: 'An engaging and lively player, a quite unusually strong and active girl, with a constitution like the proverbial ostrich, who scarcely knew what it was to be tired and never was sick or sorry.'

Muriel Robb, at 24, had youth on her side but little experience of the big time and had never appeared in a Wimbledon final of any kind. Her main strength was a formidable forehand and she used an overhead serve while many of the lady players were still delivering underhand. She had, too, the gritty determination of the Geordie race.

When the match commenced on Tuesday 1 July, reigning champion Mrs Sterry took the first set but was made to battle harder than she was generally accustomed to. She prevailed

6–4 but 'each game was well contested', wrote *The Times*.

Time to draw on the ostrich constitution, perhaps. But even ageing ostriches lose their kick eventually. Miss Robb played like a demon and 'by sticking hard to her game won the second set by 13 games to 11, the closeness of the play being such that the set occupied more than three quarters of an hour'.

Now the position was tailor-made for the younger player: 'She was obviously wearing her opponent down,' said the match report. Then came the defining moment – it poured with rain and play was suspended for the day.

Needing just one set to wrest the title from the Ealing-born champion's grasp, Miss Robb's prospects looked hopeful. Over three sets Mrs Sterry might generally be regarded as favourite, but in a one-off sudden death scenario anything might happen.

Quite why the Wimbledon committee did what they did remains a mystery. Perhaps there was a touch of Home Counties' bias. They decided to replay the final in its entirety the next day.

Again it proved a battle, with Miss Robb grinding out the first set to prevail 7–5. At last Charlotte Sterry's legendary resolve faltered as she flopped 6–1 in the second set.

Muriel Robb is the only lady ever to have been called upon to win three sets in a Wimbledon final. The 53 games played remains the record for the ladies' final and the only time a replay has ever been implemented.

It seems Muriel Evelyn Robb secured her unique record in the nick of time. She never appeared at Wimbledon again and died in 1907, aged just 28.

As for the ostrich, maybe the pen pictures were right after all. After several more near-misses she became champion again in 1908 at the age of 37 years and 282 days, still the oldest ever for the ladies' singles. No doubt she was still telling the tale when she died at 96.

NOT MUCH KOPTER TENNIS

LONDON, AUGUST 1903

Sir,
You were good enough to allow me to propose to deal in
your columns with a new ball game. It belongs to a genus
which includes lawn tennis and other games of its kind and
from an incident in the game has been called 'Kopter
Tennis'.

Thus Oswald Crawfurd began his long epistle to the editor of
The Times on 29 August 1903.

Gadgets, inventions, novelties and sundry bizarre, mostly
entirely unworkable, ideas were something of an obsession
with men of the Victorian and Edwardian age. Sports and
games were a popular field for the creative mind.

Ever since Major Walter Clopton Wingfield had patented
his game of Sphairistike in 1874 and promoted it with such
vigour that it evolved into the huge phenomenon of lawn
tennis, others with an eye for a fast buck had sought to emulate
his success.

The *Eastbourne Gazette* for July 1883 waxed lyrical on the
charms of the new game of Hildegarde, a curious hybrid of
tennis, rounders and cricket; it sank without trace. A decade
later a game called Five-Ten, a cross, surprise surprise,
between fives and tennis attempted to seduce the public; it
sank without trace.

In 1895 there was an abortive attempt to introduce lawn

55

football, played on a court 50 feet long by 20 feet wide divided by a net over which the ball could only be kicked or headed.

Nor did the brilliantly innovative motor car polo and stilt-soccer quite catch on at the start of the twentieth century.

But Oswald Crawfurd knew, with that innate sense of destiny and certainty born entirely from self-deluded eccentricity, that Kopter Tennis would eclipse lawn tennis completely.

Alas for Crawfurd, his new game never knew what it was to grow old. It joined other sporting denizens of the deep by going down without even a splash.

A close scrutiny of Crawfurd's flawed rationale and complicated rules make the reasons for its failure quickly apparent. 'Lawn tennis consists of little more than the returning of a ball over a net,' asserted Crawfurd. 'Moreover, the elasticity of the ball and the strength and drive of the racquet have quite outgrown the court to such a degree that even lawn tennis on a court half as large again would hardly be too large. The game has in consequence deteriorated.'

Although there was a large consensus of public agreement in Crawfurd's observation that, just as we say today, tennis had become too powerful, it was simply too popular a game to yield to any usurper. Something ought to have told Crawfurd that those curious white-lined rectangles, which could be seen almost anywhere in the world, meant that tennis had taken hold.

Crawfurd still persisted: 'The court for Kopter is one-third the size of a lawn court and the gut-strung racquet is replaced by a small wooden bat covered with felt while the ball, of hollow India-rubber covered in cloth, shall not exceed one and nine-sixteenths of an inch or be less than one and seven-sixteenths in diameter.' So far, so good, maybe. Crawfurd, it seems, had invented 'short tennis', the value of which to young players is undisputed today.

But regrettably he over-egged the pudding in his court layout and scoring system. To describe the game in full here would be impossible; the rain forests are just too valuable a resource.

A couple of tasters will suffice:

The net is 26 inches high and in each court division and on the same side is a net three yards in length and 26 inches in height carried by a rod running from the extreme point of the central net and ending, towards the base of the court, in a curve having a diameter of 12 inches with its opening 6 inches wide. The side nets are on the boundary lines of the court, stretched out by rods and having curves corresponding to the supporting rods and the circle formed in each court division by the lower of the two rods whose bending forms the side of the net is the chace.

About on a par for entertainment with putting together a self-assembly bookcase? Naturally there would always be one rod left over. So to the scoring:

The game is 20 up and the points are made or lost by faults, by failure to return the ball, by 'inset' strokes by 'chaces' and by penalties. If either player so strikes the ball that when dead it lies within the inset space, then three points are scored. A chace is made by a ball which enters and remains in the chace circle and counts six points but if during the ensuing rally the striker's adversary also makes a chace, then the first chace is off.

That is a mere fraction of Crawfurd's pitch to the readers of *The Times*. He signed off by saying that the game had been thoroughly tested at his home at 34, Hans Road, Hans Place, London SW and that the laws, diagrams, sectional views of the court and the equipment could be had from Messrs Buchanan at 15 Pall Mall. Finally, he invited readers to respond.

Over the ensuing weeks many letters were sent to the editor, all of them about the price of corn.

Kopter Tennis must surely be the oddest version of tennis ever invented and the strangest game of tennis *never* played. Thank goodness for Major Wingfield.

HEADS OR TAILS?

WORPLE ROAD, WIMBLEDON, 1904

No one in the game denies that there have always been the occasional 'contrived results'.

Players injured, feeling under the weather, with a plane to catch or maybe a hot date lined up, have sometimes felt obliged to give the public a match without having any real desire to win it. Most of the time the audiences never knew, but one contrivance, arguably the oddest of all time, was perpetrated in a much more public way.

It was Wimbledon 1904 when the British players Frank Riseley and Sydney Smith, partners in the doubles, found themselves drawn against each other in the semi-finals of the All Comers' singles.

They were also doing rather well in the doubles and were on their way to the All Comers' final of that, with the chance of reaching the Challenge Final where the redoubtable holders, the Doherty brothers, awaited them.

Neither Riseley nor Smith fancied a long singles semi so it was with some chagrin that they saw their 'play fair' approach take them to two sets all at 7–5, 5–7, 8–6, 5–7. Either player might have thrown the decider with some judicious hitting wide of the lines but it just wasn't British to do it that way. After a short consultation, they reached a novel and unprecedented conclusion. They decided to dispense with the fifth set altogether and toss a coin for the match.

Thus it was that Frank Riseley, in the interests of energy

conservation, became the only player to reach a Wimbledon All Comers' final on the toss of a coin. The ruse looked to have worked as he then advanced to the Challenge Final with an easy 6–0, 6–1, 6–2 win over M. J. G. Ritchie.

But he didn't have recourse to the toss of a coin on Monday 27 June as Laurie Doherty won the third of his five in a row in the Challenge Finals by 6–1, 7–5, 8–6.

Nor did Smith and Riseley pull it off two days later in the Challenge Round of the doubles – this time it was Laurie and his brother Reggie Doherty who did the joint damage, 6–3, 6–4, 6–3.

It was, surely, a deserved comeuppance for the two most famous tossers in lawn tennis history who'd denied the paying public a fight to the finish.

Yet Riseley and Smith are by no means the only players to have agreed a result under the full gaze of public scrutiny.

It was just over 50 years later that the American J. E. 'Budge' Patty met Jaroslav Drobny, born in Prague but playing under Egyptian nationality, in an indoor professional final in Lyon.

Both players might have been excused for regarding it as 'just another game' for time and again the two had played each other on the professional touring circuit, travelling from city to city, each time playing to a different audience who expected the action to be fast and furious, fresh and hard fought, all at the same time.

Finals night at the Lyon Indoor Professional Tournament ought to have been no different from any other on paper but the score that resulted from the scheduled five-setter remains one of the great oddities in tennis history: a draw!

They say that familiarity breeds contempt but it also, in tennis, breeds an inbuilt mutual anticipation of what a regular opponent is going to do at any given time. Winning points becomes increasingly tricky and long rallies are par for the course.

Drobny took the first set 21–19. Patty won the second by a mere 10–8. By the time they reached 21–21 in the third the spectators had been thoroughly entertained and absorbed for 4 hours 35 minutes but might also have been wondering what time they would get home to bed.

Already the players had notched up 100 games and, with a set to conclude and another two possibly to come, it looked like 150 games or so could be on the cards, possibly many more. That would have been an all-time record to this day.

But the good people of Lyon did get to their beds that night, thanks to the understanding that existed between Patty and Drobny. Common sense prevailed as they drew the line at 100, walked to the net, shook hands and called it quits, to register one of just a handful of draws recorded in the tennis archives.

An honourable end or a dishonourable one? It's a matter for debate.

In 1904, Riseley and Smith showed one way of choosing the winner and loser. In 1955, Patty and Drobny didn't even bother with 'heads or tails?'

BRITAIN TAKES THE MEDALS

OLYMPIC GAMES, LONDON, JULY 1908

Since the Modern Olympic Games began in 1896, the number of occasions on which British competitors have made a clean sweep of the medals in one event has been, let's admit it, rather fewer than they would have liked.

So hats off to the British ladies' tennis squad at the 1908 London Olympics who saw off all opposition to take gold, silver and bronze. What a proud moment it must have been as the long-skirted heroines ran down every ball and rallied to the cause, pink cheeks all aglow, with true British spirit.

But alas, behind this most agreeable 1–2–3 is a rather different story.

What could possibly be insinuated? Might it have been a hollow victory? Who were the opposition? In truth, a more appropriate question is 'Where was the opposition?' Let the farce commence.

Matters began only mildly strangely when it was decided there would be two Olympic lawn tennis titles that year, a covered court tournament staged at Queen's Club in May, followed by a contest on grass at Wimbledon in July.

Gladys Eastlake Smith served notice of Britain's triumphal intentions by taking the indoor gold and two months later the grass court Olympics sprang into action at Wimbledon's Worple Road ground.

'Sprang' may be too strong a word. Teetered proved to be about right. Thirteen ladies put their names forward for entry into the singles, among them six overseas players willing to mix it with the seven-strong British field. But things started to go pear-shaped early on.

Officials in charge of the draw squirmed uneasily as none of the overseas players turned up! They comforted themselves with the thought that it could still be a cracking contest even though Britain was guaranteed the medals. It was, after all, a strong field.

There was Charlotte Sterry, fresh from winning her fifth Wimbledon crown the month before, and six-times champion Blanche Hillyard; what a battle that might be. 'Might' proved to be the operative word as both of them scratched. The officials, meanwhile, merely began to itch a little.

'Nil desperandum!' they cried. That still left five fine players chasing those three elusive medals. It was fighting talk but nothing more as the destination of gold, silver and bronze was decided by playing just four matches in four rounds.

In a ludicrous draw, which included all eight phantom players, walkovers were the order of the day. Madame Fenwick, the French hope, was entirely conspicuous by her absence but still progressed to the semi-final draw by first 'defeating' the equally invisible Austrian torch-bearer Miss Matouch and following this walkover with another over fellow truant Charlotte Sterry.

While Madame Fenwick might have read of her disembodied Olympic progress with not a little astonishment from the comfort of a sun-drenched terrace somewhere on the French Riviera, Dorothea Katharine Lambert-Chambers, 'Dolly' to her chums, born in Ealing and British as they come, seized gold by winning three matches comfortably.

At least she sang for her supper even if no one else did. Her opponent in the final was Dora Boothby, who just about made a game of it by losing 6–1, 7–5 after getting there without striking a ball, courtesy of two walkovers. Thus she became the honoured recipient of an Olympic silver medal without winning a match and by taking only six games.

Even that performance was heroic compared to the one that captured the bronze; that coveted gong went to Ruth Winch whose only match was her semi-final defeat against Lambert-Chambers in which she took the measly total of two games.

No matter! It was a triple triumph for the British who had steadfastly overcome the absentee Austrian, French and Hungarian entrants by adhering to the most important principle of lawn tennis competition. The cynics may chorus 'It's a lottery' and that's precisely the point.

Those British girls weren't daft. They knew the first rule of any competition. If you're not in it you can't win it.

It might have been the hollowest tennis victory of all time but who cares? Well played, ladies!

A SHORT-LIVED AFFAIR

NOTTINGHAM, JULY 1912

The official Laws of Tennis have always been clear enough, but there are Unwritten Laws too. As every tennis club member knows, Unwritten Law No. 1, which has been in existence ever since the birth of the game, goes as follows:

> A gentleman engaging in mixed doubles play shall under no circumstances partner his wife, fiancée, girlfriend or other person to whom he is affectionately attached without having first signed an agreement not to argue, bicker, scoff, mutter inaudibly, stare dolefully or otherwise belittle said partner before, during or after the course of play. This is in the interests of the ongoing amicable preservation of such relationships and out of consideration for opponents who may be acutely embarrassed by such altercations as may occur.

Perhaps better still, just to avoid it altogether, but no one seems to have alerted Mrs G. W. Hillyard to that possibility, for it was she who brazenly flouted good common sense to institute the most unlikely competition in lawn tennis history, the All England Married Couples' Championship.

The idea first struck her back in 1910 while playing a friendly married foursomes at the Newcastle Club in that beautiful and somewhat secret area of Nottingham known as The Park, where tennis is still played today. The committee

64

jumped at the idea and tagged the event on to the Nottinghamshire Championships.

Mrs Hillyard, winner of the Wimbledon singles six times from 1886 to 1900, duly took the title on that first occasion with hubby Commander George Whiteside Hillyard, himself a Wimbledon doubles champion but best known as secretary of the All England Club from 1907 to 24.

In 1911, they lifted the trophy again and when it came to Saturday 20 July 1912 they were told that a hat trick would entitle them to the cup outright. This they secured by a 9–7, 7–5 victory over Dr and Mrs Lamplough, all accomplished apparently without the exchange of a single harsh word or withering glance. Then again they hadn't endured too much pressure as they'd had a bye to the final – only four couples from the whole of England entered, and one of those scratched. Perhaps, also, after 25 years of marriage, they had an understanding. Certainly it was smiles all round as the committee presented them not only with the trophy but a beautiful piece of Sheffield plate as a silver wedding gift.

The Hillyards were, it seems, an exception to the rule. During the entire history of the competition the largest entry was five couples. After the 1923 tournament the committee decided that an amicable annulment might be the best course of action. Including a break for the First World War, when it was cancelled altogether, the competition was held just nine times.

The Married Couples' Championships remains the most short-lived and least-entered of the All England titles and there are no plans to revive it. The cause has been cited as 'irretrievable breakdown'.

ONE IN THE EYE FOR THE LADIES

WORPLE ROAD, WIMBLEDON, JULY 1913

It was the Irish who started it. The first serious competition for ladies was the Irish Championships of 1879 in Dublin and it was one of their own, the spirited and rather rebellious May Langrishe, who lifted this major trophy in ladies' competition.

Langrishe's feisty temperament was unusual and other ladies of spirit who did play tennis had to fight hard to throw off the rather delicate image that some of their colleagues presented.

Thirty-four years on, as Wimbledon 1913 prepared to start, they'd just about cracked it and Emmeline Pankhurst and her fellow suffragettes had helped no end by playing the strong-women card to solid effect.

Maybe it was the number 13 that did it but the unusual events at that year's Wimbledon gave the male chauvinists a renewed opportunity to re-assert their authority and chortle at the ladies' expense.

The male mutterings started at the gates when for the first time bags and parcels were closely scrutinized by doormen as a consequence of a suffragette raid on the grounds earlier in the year.

As if that wasn't enough, fans who favoured the men's game were aghast to learn that both the mixed and ladies' doubles competitions, hitherto regarded as light-hearted side issues, had been upgraded into official championship events.

It was the perfect chance for the fairer sex to show their

66

mettle but one they ended up blowing at the final hurdle.

Again it was the Irish who started it during the mixed doubles final on Thursday 3 July. Reigning singles champion Ethel Larcombe had a strong partner in Irish rugby international Cecil Parke and they raced into a lead by taking the first set 6–3 against Agnes Tuckey and the determined Hope Crisp, later famed for continuing to play good tennis after the war when handicapped by an artificial leg.

The Times observed that 'Parke then found himself in an erratic mood and was particularly at fault with his smashing, the ball finally flying off his racket at an angle and striking Mrs Larcombe a severe blow in the eye.' She duly retired hurt at 6–3, 3–5. One final down, two to go.

So unnerved was our Ethel by the incident, though, that she promptly withdrew from the singles Challenge Round in which she should have met Mrs Lambert-Chambers. The ladies' showcase event therefore became a walkover and sections of the male tennis following began to scoff. Surely these ladies just weren't up to the mark. Two finals down, one to go.

So to the ladies' doubles, the last chance for them to show some real resilience. On Friday 4 July, the climax to the meeting, Charlotte Sterry and Mrs Lambert-Chambers led Dora Boothby and Winnie McNair 6–4, 4–2 when 'Chattie' pulled up sharply. She pulled out of the match equally sharply bemoaning an injured tendon. Three finals down, none to go.

So, not one of the events involving the ladies were completed. In the very year the fairer sex ought to have finally come of age, injuries had put paid to all three finals.

The reporter from *The Times*, male of course, might just have been making mischief in his final summing up. He simply wrote: 'And in this miserable fashion closed what has been in many ways the most successful tournament Wimbledon has ever known.'

THE SURVIVOR

WORPLE ROAD, WIMBLEDON, JULY 1920

'A real survivor.' A term used in life and sport and particularly in tennis, where hanging on in there is a quality that every champion needs. Norris Williams was one such real survivor.

On Saturday 3 July 1920 this tall willowy American, born in Geneva, Switzerland, in 1891, but later naturalized as a US citizen, walked on to the Centre Court at Worple Road, Wimbledon, to contest the gentlemen's doubles final. His partner was Pittsburgh-born Charles Garland and their opponents were the British pair A. R. F. Kingscote and James Parke.

Most of the crowd knew all about J. C. Parke, not simply for his previous Wimbledon success in the mixed doubles in 1914 but also on account of his all-round prowess as a sportsman. He was a scratch golfer and had been capped 20 times by Ireland as a rugby international, captaining them on three occasions. Whoever dishes out the talent had been generous with the helpings when Parke entered this world; maybe the initials J. C. got him noticed.

Kingscote, too, was a stalwart sort of fellow, born in Bangalore, India, and glorying in the Christian names Algernon Robert Fitzhardinge. He was a classic product of the British Empire and could be relied upon not to yield lightly to the much younger American pairing.

As for the Americans, little had been seen of them but they had been massively hyped by the press in advance of their

68

arrival, coming as part of the Davis Cup team which would take on Great Britain after Wimbledon.

The Americans were both delighted and relieved to have arrived safely at the home of tennis because their ship had been delayed and it was only by the good offices of the US Secretary of War that they got here at all. They crossed the Atlantic on the US army transport vessel *Northern Pacific*. Norris Williams, who shall we say was an experienced sailor, didn't turn a hair.

As the doubles competition had progressed, it became evident that Williams and Garland must have some clout, for they beat their higher-profile compatriots, the two 'Bills', Tilden and Johnston, in a classic five-set semi-final.

So to the All Comers' final which, in 1920, would decide the doubles title itself because the previous year's winners had not come back to defend their crown in the Challenge Round.

No American pairing had ever won the Wimbledon men's doubles in its 32-year history, but Williams and Garland broke through that exclusion zone to put the sterling silver Challenge Cup into US hands for the first time.

The match was a tight one, Kingscote and Parke taking the first set 6–4, but the American pair rattled off the next three sets in fine style, 6–4, 7–5, 6–2. The doyen of tennis journalists, A. Wallis Myers, recorded the victory thus: 'Williams and Garland triumphed as much by their service returns and ground strokes in the rallies as by their service and volleying. They were, in short, more British in their methods than American, though they imported dash and agility.' How comforting to know that, even in defeat, British methods won the day. As for the evidently revolutionary dash and agility, a certain Fred Perry would get the hang of it 14 years later.

So, I hear you ask, Where is the strangeness? The Americans broke the stranglehold . . . so what? Was there a remarkable incident in the game? One has to admit, there wasn't. Except, perhaps, that one of the players might never have been there at all.

Richard Norris Williams, Harvard educated, US army veteran of the First World War and winner of the Croix de

Guerre, carried a secret few in the crowd were aware of.

What really made Norris Williams and this match unique in tennis history was an experience that befell him when he was just 21. Shortly before midnight on 14 April 1912 he went for a swim in a big pool otherwise known as the Atlantic Ocean. He swam in ice-cold water for over an hour before a friendly soul suggested he might like rescuing. Other people, 1,490 of them, including his own father, weren't so lucky and would never get the chance to match Norris Williams's record, one that can never be beaten.

He is the only survivor of the sinking of the *Titanic* ever to have won a Wimbledon title.

Norris Williams died aged 78 in Bryn Mawr, Pennsylvania, USA, on 2 June 1968 but he will always be the greatest survivor in tennis history.

ONE OVERHEAD TOO MANY

FOREST HILLS, NEW YORK, SEPTEMBER 1920

Forest Hills has seen some dramatic action in its illustrious history, but nothing to match what happened on Monday 6 September 1920 in the US Championships final between great friends and rivals Bill Tilden and Bill Johnston.

Many rank Philadelphia-born 'Big Bill' Tilden the best player the world has ever seen. He was a slow starter, taking his first major title at the ripe old age of 27 when he won the 1920 Wimbledon, but was never to look back from there.

Californian 'Little Bill' Johnston was a year younger than Tilden but had already won the US title in 1915 and again in 1919 when Big Bill had been his victim.

Could Tilden gain revenge to win his first US crown? The press dubbed the match the 'Battle for the World Championship' as America's tennis fans held their breath.

Sure enough there were gasps galore as the games fluctuated but it was for astonishing events off court that this contest has entered the realms of the ultra-bizarre.

Under grey, forbidding skies, everything started so normally and the 10,000-strong crowd in the wooden Centre Court stands saw Tilden cruise the first set 6–1, using his much–improved backhand drive to stunning effect. In the second set, Johnston fought back equally emphatically, exploiting the lob ruthlessly to expose Tilden's weakest stroke, his overhead.

As the eyes of the crowd looked skyward time and again, Tilden faltered and Johnston took the set 6–1.

It was entertaining stuff, but not yet a classic, so the crowd were pleased enough to again look skyward at the start of the third to watch a small two-seater plane flying above, for flying, and stunting in particular, was the great new craze. At the controls of the one-engined JN–Curtiss was Navy Lieutenant James Murray Grier and sitting behind him was an army photographer, Sergeant Joseph Saxe.

As they took off from Mitchel Field in Garden City nearby on Long Island, their mission was a routine one – to take aerial shots of the tennis final to use in a forces recruitment campaign. 'Join the army and have fun!' was the gist of things.

Grier flew over at 500 feet and the crowd were amused when Saxe popped up from his seat to take his shots. Tilden and Johnston gave withering upward glances and for his next pass the pilot rose to 900 feet. That didn't please Saxe, who wanted to get in closer for his shots, so on his third run Grier came in at just 300 feet. Even the spectators now showed their annoyance and fists were waved skyward as Grier came in for his fourth pass at only 400 feet.

When he rose for his fifth approach both crowd and players must have wished he'd call it a day but when they heard the engine stall and saw the plane start a graceful arc of a descent they were convinced Grier had started a stunt routine.

But Grier's battle with the controls was no stunt – it was a fight for his and Saxe's life, a fight he failed to win. Up went the tail before the final sickeningly silent vertical plummet into a vacant plot of land just 200 yards behind the stand. The crowd knew as they heard the crushing impact that both men would be dead. Bill Tilden later said he 'felt the court tremor' beneath his feet.

There was no precedent for procedure and as some of the ghoulish elements of the crowd left their seats for a close look, famous umpire E. C. Conlin, fearing a panic, quietly asked Johnston and Tilden, 'Can you go on?'

Both players nodded and remarkably proceeded to produce what one New York reporter described as 'mechanically perfect tennis amid incredible drama, with the crowd exhibiting a mob spirit and not above razzing the officials'.

Tilden took the third set 7–5 and moved ahead to match point in the fourth at 5–4. Again the crowd looked skyward, this time at the gathering gloom and, at the precise moment Tilden served, the heavens opened and the crowd stirred noisily. Tilden turned away from Johnston's return, assuming umpire Conlin would call a 'let' for the commotion, which he did. But as the players left the court for a rain break, referee George Adee was already over-ruling Conlin and giving the point to Johnston.

Tilden was furious on his return, arguing for a full five minutes and becoming so distracted that he served three double faults in a row, Johnston going on to take the set 7–5.

All square. Now for the finale. Tilden prevailed 6–3 in the fifth to take the match. Some of the press called it 'the greatest final in US tennis history' but no one could deny that the tragedy in the skies had overshadowed the occasion.

As Tilden shook Johnston's hand as the newly crowned Champion of the World, the crumpled bodies of Grier and Saxe were being extricated from the mangled wreckage.

WELL SMASHED, SIR!

WORPLE ROAD, WIMBLEDON, JUNE 1921

The championships of 1921 occupy a special place in Wimbledon history, as the last held at the original Worple Road ground before the move, necessitated by ever-increasing crowds, to the present Church Road. Two legends of the game, America's Bill Tilden and France's Suzanne Lenglen, took the singles titles to give the bulging grounds a memorable send-off.

But many would recall this championships for a men's singles quarter-final, a curious encounter which positively fizzed with interest.

Birmingham-born, but Australian-bred, Randolph Lycett was the best British player of the early 1920s, three times winner of both the men's and mixed doubles, an individualistic and dogged fighter.

Facing him was crowd and press favourite Zenzo Shimidzu, 'the little Japanese', noted for his scurrying play, unorthodox style and trademark pork-pie hat.

It was the middle Saturday, 25 June. The crowds were huge and it was swelteringly hot. *The Times* correspondent noted 'how trying were the conditions on the Centre Court where the stands reflect the heat and keep off any breeze'. Lycett and Shimidzu entered the cauldron.

Now it needs to be understood before progressing this tale that the statutory rest period between games, which today's players enjoy as of right, had not then been instituted. Indeed chairs for players to sit on weren't introduced at Wimbledon until 1975.

Although in the States there was a more relaxed attitude to breaks, the British way was, as *The Times* explained, simply to keep going: 'In England the game is supposed to be played without break from start to finish though it is an accepted convention that a player may wipe his brow or moisten his gullet as he passes the umpire's chair.' Not only was Randolph Lycett ready to flout the no-break convention but he was also about to take the gullet-moistening to unprecedented degrees.

Shimidzu took the first set 6–3. Lycett took the next two 11–9 and 6–3. It was then that the heat began to tell on 35-year-old Lycett, but like all good sportsmen he knew what to do. Take plenty of fluid.

Unfortunately, as the *Daily Telegraph* reported with some indignation, his choice of fluid was a touch unwise: 'Lycett broke all precedent by bringing a "trainer" on to the Centre Court, equipped with champagne.'

Oh dear! The effects were not surprising. As rampant dehydration further heightened Lycett's thirst he called for even more champagne, borne on to court by a liveried waiter hailed from the tea lawn.

Although the temperature soared, there was, as it were, a distinct nip in the air, and it wasn't the little Japanese rising for a smash. As the alcohol took effect, Lycett's game assumed an interesting air. Freed from all traces of nerves he frequently won points with relaxed strokes but at other times, as another newspaper report noted, 'Mr Lycett's distress was obvious. He was still capable of making powerful smashes but fell over several times when trying to turn sharply.'

Lycett lost the fourth set 6–2. 'Tired and emotional' as he was, the last thing he needed was a marathon decider. But he got it all the same. The bubbly imbibing continued and he was also seen sipping from a flask which some said contained brandy. Gin was also mentioned in dispatches.

The rests between games became longer. As 'treatment' was administered, the crowd, although largely turning a blind eye, became a little restless and murmurs began to circulate around the court. Shimidzu remained inscrutable. 'In the last set all one noticed were the delays but no sign of impatience escaped Mr Shimidzu as he waited with polite concern while applications internal and external were administered to Mr Lycett,' wrote a reporter the next day.

Remarkably Lycett had two match points for what would have been a famous victory. In the event, it was an equally famous defeat as he finally succumbed 10–8 in the fifth. For Randolph though, this proved merely a hiccup, as a few days later he stormed to victory, stone-cold sober, in both the men's and mixed doubles finals.

Just as extraordinary as Lycett's hazy performance itself was the hazy way in which the press reported the transparently alcoholic content of his singles débâcle. While *The Times* condemned Lycett's 'blatant disregard of the spirit of the game' they summed up euphemistically by saying that 'the sun, one has to assume, had much to do with his defeat'. Today's tabloids would surely scream 'Randy smashed as he loses his bottle'.

Lycett died in Jersey in February 1935, aged only 48. There was, fittingly, an 'unconscious' tribute to him at the Championships preceding his death when all Centre Court competitors were able to avail themselves of a new Wimbledon innovation – 13 years too late for Randolph Lycett, Robinson's Lemon Barley Water made its long-awaited entrance.

TENNIS OF THE ABSURD

UNITED STATES, 1925

Tennis hit new heights in the Roaring Twenties when the austerity and restrictions of war could finally be forgotten and doing your own thing was all the rage.

That must have been what Ivan Runger and Gladys Roy had in mind when they faced each other for a man *v.* woman tennis showdown in 1925, for this was no ordinary game.

For a start the court was rather smaller than standard; 16 feet by a measly 4 didn't leave much room for manoeuvre but at least covering the baseline wasn't a problem.

As for spectators there was a capacity crowd of just two men and one of those had a restricted view seat, not surprising as it was actually underneath the court.

The net was 2 feet high and the court surface, although firm, had a curious camber which would surely make control difficult. Added to that, the incessant crosswind blew so fiercely that both players supplemented their immaculate white attire with goggles.

There was, too, a constant and annoying noise, which made concentration well nigh impossible.

But with their rackets poised neither player seemed too concerned about chasing a swirling ball. That might have been because neither of them could run – both players' feet were firmly shackled to the court. Then again it might equally have been because there wasn't a tennis ball in sight. They had agreed to play with invisible ones.

77

The game commenced. As Runger eased himself into a well-balanced forehand, confident that it was a shot he really couldn't miss, his female opponent squatted low, rocking from side to side, equally certain that she would make a solid return. These days we would call it performance art. This was tennis beyond strangeness. Never has there been a more absurd version of the game or a more unusual location. Unlikely as it may sound, but for an anonymous American photographer recording the event for posterity, this most singular of singles might never have been verified.

It is one of the great tennis action shots, and so succinctly titled: 'Ivan Runger and Gladys Roy Playing Tennis on Wings of an Aeroplane in Flight.'

ONE HELL OF A WARM UP!

REIGATE, JULY 1925

What could epitomize the essence of English tennis better than a club tournament in beautiful Home Counties Surrey in the elegant 1920s? One can almost taste those cucumber sandwiches.

As the lawn tennis loungers and dizzy young flappers of the charming medieval market town of Reigate looked forward to their annual tournament at Manor Road, all was right with the world and only the weather, if it dared, might dampen the spirits.

The weeks before opening day had been pleasantly hot and the grass courts were perfectly hard and dry. Fingers crossed for Monday 13 July.

The tennis gods smiled on Reigate Lawn Tennis Club that day and every tournament organizer's worst nightmare, a badly interrupted first day, was blissfully avoided. The men's and ladies' singles advanced apace without stoppage.

What would the next day bring? The forecast for Tuesday 14 July was encouraging: 'Mainly fair. Light, variable winds. Warm,' read the weather column in the morning papers.

Tournament organizer Hamilton Price must have breakfasted contentedly that morning. All was going so well.

The forecast was spot on and, as play commenced, Reigate LTC must have presented a glorious green and white vision to the passengers who now and again waved cheerily from the passing trains. The noise could be a mite irritating if it caught

79

one in mid-serve but, lest we forget, these were the grand old days of steam and they added, surely, to the charm of the occasion.

It was bound to happen one day. If there is a patron saint of tennis tournaments, and there ought to be, he was evidently in a mischievous mood. *The Times* report was succinct: 'Sparks from a passing train set fire to grass on an embankment adjoining the courts of the Reigate LTC and play in the tournament was suspended for some time.'

The light variable winds (for the forecasters had for once been super-accurate) playfully did their stuff and gently fanned the flames to spread the mayhem. The fire brigade was duly called out, all bells clanging. Reigate had not seen such excitement in many a long year.

'Warm' it most certainly was. It is pleasing to report that play did resume, the tournament was completed and there were no casualties, not even the unluckiest tournament organizer of all time who, it is believed, survived with sanity intact to start all over again the following year.

A few words of comfort to Hamilton Price might be appropriate. The uneasy relationship between lawn tennis and fire is not entirely confined to Reigate. Amongst a number of recorded incidents are the small fire in the Centre Court stands at Wimbledon in 1932 and on Saturday 26 June 1999, play on Court 18 was suspended as a precautionary measure as smoke billowed ominously from a substantial fire in a nearby block of flats.

Perhaps the most spectacular fire incident, though, belongs to the Foro Italico in Rome, all the more bizarre because of its deliberate nature. When the red clay there gets too wet, the organizers have been known to *flambé* the courts by dousing them in petrol and setting them alight.

Reigate's Hamilton Price would surely have cast a damper over those proceedings.

THE SHOWDOWN

CANNES, SOUTH OF FRANCE, FEBRUARY 1926

It's been labelled the 'Battle of the Century' and in terms of pure glamour, hype and media interest there's surely never been a match to compare with the extraordinary head to head between the temperamental French diva Suzanne Lenglen and the poker-faced challenger from the United States, Helen Wills.

In the jazz-age 1920s, when tennis players really were stars and the stylish French Riviera their favourite stage, the 'Divine Suzanne' was the undisputed 'Empress of the Côte d'Azur'. Season after season between 1919 and 1925 she'd left her base in Nice with her ever-present entourage, Mama, Papa and their irritating little dog Gyp, to sweep the board in the tennis world.

Only once in that time had she 'lost' a singles, and that to Norwegian-American Molla Mallory in a match in which Lenglen quit when behind, 'feeling unwell' in the second set. That spoilsport propensity for crying *'j'abandonne'* when her game occasionally faltered, coupled with a general air of superiority, certainly made her some enemies among the players. The Americans, in particular, were keen to produce a challenger who would beat her fair and square.

Enter the young pretender, 20-year-old Californian Helen Wills, who had never played Lenglen but was dispatching opponents decisively enough to be declared lady-in-waiting. When Wills announced her intention to play the Riviera spring circuit, a clash in Lenglen's own back yard looked inevitable.

Pressmen who had never covered tennis before were sent from the States to 'get that story' and ludicrous fees were paid to some celebrity authors to do likewise as experienced writers and hacks alike converged on the South of France early in 1926.

But Lenglen kept the media circus waiting. At the Hotel Metropole event in Cannes she refused to enter the singles. In week two at Gallia she pulled out again as 'Papa was ill'. She did enter for Nice in week three but Wills, by this time herself well irritated, withdrew in a fit of pique.

As the press waited and expense claims mounted as rapidly as the tension, the two stars eventually entered the same tournament, fully four weeks into the tour, at the famous Carlton Hotel in Cannes. Just to prolong the agony, the heavens opened for a whole four days before both players mercifully reached the final amidst interest now amounting to frenzy.

At 11 am on Tuesday 16 February 1926 the appointed hour finally arrived. So too did Lenglen, wearing a fur-trimmed white coat, full warpaint and a regal smile, waving graciously from her chauffeured limo to the heaving and neck-craning crowds.

At the arena itself, really nothing more than a court in the hotel gardens, workmen still hammered on a temporary stand, men perched atop a garage, and others removed tiles from their house roofs and poked their heads through for a free view. A few small boys perched in the branches of a eucalyptus tree until the police ejected them and promptly colonized the branches themselves.

The posh seats were awash with finery as business tycoons mingled with some of the world's top nobs: the former King Manoel of Portugal, Grand Duke Michael of Russia, Prince George of Greece, the Duke of Westminster and the Rajah and Ranee of Pudukota just for starters.

There were no American or French linesmen. Papa Lenglen and the Wills entourage had both insisted on complete impartiality, so the Brits took charge.

The scene was set as 4,000 spectators watched the red clay from every vantage point. In truth the match itself did not live up to the hype as Lenglen, sipping brandy from a silver flask between games, won the first set 6–3 and advanced to match point at 6–5 in the second.

In a Hollywood film there would have been a big, unbelievable ending. Strangely enough, as if scripted, the showdown didn't disappoint.

On match point Wills hit close to the line and the call of 'out' was clearly heard. As the players shook hands a linesman signalled frantically that it had been a spectator's call, not his. The point was given to Wills, the match restarted and Lenglen lost that game. Who knows what story would have unfolded if she'd lost the match? Quite possibly an on-court suicide!

In the event Lenglen held her nerve to take the set 8–6. Ever dramatic, she celebrated victory by collapsing on to a courtside bench in floods of tears as she all but disappeared under the huge floral tributes thrust towards her as the French fans went wild.

Could a Hollywood scriptwriter have bettered it? Dare he have written that the fates would decree that the two would never meet in a singles match again? They never did.

Or could he have penned a more fantastic ending for the vanquished Helen than reality provided? As she forlornly left the court a young man leapt the barrier, forcing his way to her side to say 'You played awfully well.'

He was Frederick Shander Moody Jr, a wealthy San Francisco stockbroker. That day Helen Wills won the prize that Suzanne, single to her death, would never capture, as three years later she married her courtside admirer and went on to win everything in sight as Helen Wills-Moody.

It was the final twist to an extraordinary day, one never to be repeated in all tennis history.

ROYAL FLUSH

WIMBLEDON, JUNE 1926

My dearest Papa,
We are both very pleased at having won the cup for the
doubles. Our hardest match was the semi-final as we lost the
first set and after winning the second set easily we only just
won the third after our opponents were 4–1 in games.

It is the sort of letter that any 11-year-old schoolboy starting at
boarding school would send to his father in an age when the
stiff upper lip and becoming a man were drilled into any young
fellow worth his salt.
The letter proceeds:

I was very surprised to get through the three rounds of singles
into the semi-finals but Greig defeated me as I knew he
would. In the doubles we nearly collapsed from fatigue and I
don't think I have ever played so well in my life. I did not lose
my head at the critical moment, which was very lucky.

This rather touching communication from a son evidently so
eager to impress his father is no ordinary letter. The 'boy',
Albert, was an RAF captain already embarked on manhood,
and the tournament was the British RAF Lawn Tennis
Championships.
The father just happened to be King George V, ruler of
Great Britain and the Empire.

This poignant letter says so much about the character of Prince Albert Frederick Arthur George, Duke of York, who would ascend the British throne himself in December 1936 as George VI.

Uncertain, lacking in confidence, eager to please . . . and keen on tennis. Bertie fought manfully against this inherent shyness in the course of fulfilling his duties and royal biographers have cited his RAF tennis victory as one of his first really public successes, something that gave him a bigger boost than anything he'd ever achieved before.

That's why, in 1926, when his RAF doubles partner Wing Commander Louis Greig suggested they might enter Wimbledon together, Prince Albert jumped at the chance with a new-found confidence. Off the court he was diffident, but on it he knew he could impress.

It was Wimbledon's Jubilee year and both King George and Queen Mary were there for a special past-champions parade on opening day. It was the highest profile championships Wimbledon had ever held.

Would the duke's game hold up under the expected close scrutiny of the public and media? Having watched him play in 1920, *The Times* correspondent seemed reasonably impressed: 'The Duke has an athlete's build and understands the principles of the game.' But does one detect an element of fudge? Could he 'play'? Dan Maskell, doyen of tennis commentators, who once ballboyed for the duke at Queen's Club, later tellingly recalled that 'his backhand was only a moderate stroke'.

The Wimbledon committee were faced with a dilemma. As an 'attraction' the duke was certainly worthy of a Centre-Court slot. But to preserve his modesty in case of a flop, might not a distant outside court be more appropriate? Then again, surely that was an insult?

The opposition, at least, seemed friendly. No ruthless hard-hitting Americans, but rather the gentlemanly pairing of Old Harrovian Arthur Wentworth Gore and upstanding solicitor Herbert Roper Barrett. Gore was 58 and Barrett 52. Fair play would surely prevail.

Without a hint of irony *The Times* reported that 'the fates have shown their loyalty to the Duke of York and Wing Commander Greig in assigning to them opponents who they might well have chosen from the list.' Do I hear muffled clearing of throats? Whether it was 'arranged' no one will ever know.

Confident, perhaps, that humiliation seemed eminently avoidable, the scheduling committee opted for Court 2, the highest-profile outside court, on Thursday 24 June. It rained.

The foursome finally made it the next day. Young onlookers might well have regarded the 'old men' with some amusement but veterans of Wimbledons long gone knew better. Gore was thrice singles champion 1901–09 and Barrett had taken the Wimbledon doubles title the same number of times. Both men were natural sportsmen keen to show they could still cut the mustard.

And hot stuff it was: 6–1, 6–3, 6–2. It was all too easy for the pair with a combined age of 110. It is the only time a member of the British royal family has ever competed in a first-class tournament.

The duke's future Wimbledon visits were as a spectator.

The fallout down the years has been that this curious match was a public humiliation for the sensitive future king, watched that day by his young wife Elizabeth, latterly the much-revered centenarian the Queen Mother. It was indeed something of an embarrassment, perhaps the most public defeat of all time, but contemporary reports suggest that the press drew a diplomatic veil over any shortcomings displayed by the 'enthusiastic left-hander'. In those discreet far-off days the papers really said very little.

As for the duke himself, his only reported remark was to the tournament referee Frank Burrow: 'I fear the Wimbledon standard is rather too good for me.'

He is not the first player to realize that, and he did, shall we say, go on to success in other fields.

His daughter Queen Elizabeth and his wife the Queen Mother could no doubt elaborate, but suffice it to say the one-time Wimbledon star was a far better monarch, father and husband than he ever was a lawn tennis player.

SLOW, SLOW, QUICK, QUICK, SLOW

CANNES, SOUTH OF FRANCE, JANUARY 1927

The problem with five-set matches is that they can sometimes drag on a bit. Even the keenest tennis fan seldom sits through five sets without slipping out for a break. Then again they can be so exciting, and when the match is between two legends of French tennis in the beautiful grounds of the Carlton Hotel at Cannes, perhaps a gripping five-setter might not be a bad thing.

Who knows quite what the expectant crowd wanted when they settled down to watch Henri Cochet play Jacques Brugnon in January 1927, but what they got was one of the most extraordinary results of all time.

Cochet and Brugnon were two of the famous Four Musketeers of French tennis who so delighted crowds in the 1920s and 1930s.

Cochet was an instinctive genius of a player whose play could rise to dizzy heights then just as quickly slip to unexpected disaster. He won the Wimbledon singles twice, the US once and the French no less than five times.

Brugnon was more of a doubles specialist, most of his early successes coming with Cochet himself so the two men knew each other's strengths and weaknesses intimately.

Saturday 22 January dawned rather grey and blustery. Spectator conditions at the Carlton Club tournament weren't ideal. Did they want a quick result or a full five-setter? In the event, they got both.

Brugnon, with some brilliant volleying, waltzed to an early lead by taking the first set 6–1. In the second, for some inexplicable reason, he stayed back far more, allowing Cochet this time to take the initiative and the set 6–1. That sort of complete reversal doesn't often happen in tennis but there was much more to come.

Cochet thrust his advantage home by walking away with the third 6–0 as Brugnon apparently went walkabout. That second hammering in a row might well have broken Brugnon's spirits but he was, after all, a musketeer, and what musketeers do when they're being attacked is go for the riposte.

With a lightning-quick counter-thrust he again came forward strongly, volleying to stunning effect to take the fourth set 6–1.

Quite what the crowd were making of this remains unrecorded. Were they seeing a classic or a mere farce? A quick game or a marathon? It was all very confusing. At two sets apiece after the silliest of scoring, they surely must have felt entitled to a real humdinger in the deciding fifth.

As it was, Cochet did the humming and dinging while Brugnon just took one big sigh and with a Gallic shrug of the shoulders proceeded to lose the clincher 6–0.

The scoreboard read 1–6, 6–1, 6–0, 1–6, 6–0 in Cochet's favour.

At just 33 games it is the shortest full five-setter in official tennis records and, although 30 games is possible, such an odd fluctuation of fortunes is unlikely to occur again.

Had Cochet and Brugnon contrived it for the fans or was it simply one of those strange things that happen when two mercurial Frenchmen meet on a tennis court?

No one will ever know, but the spectators got a memorable five-setter and, what's more, lots of them saw every single point.

TILDEN'S SPEED RECORD

MANCHESTER, JUNE 1927

Bill Tilden dominated men's tennis so masterfully in the 1920s that many still rate him as the best player of all time. As world No. 1 from 1920 to 1925 and US No. 1 ten years in a row 1920 to 1929, Big Bill swept aside opponent after opponent with his cannonball serve, pace, accuracy and an acute technical and tactical awareness.

Many egos were shattered at the hands of Tilden, perhaps none more completely than that of British player D. M. Greig.

When America agreed to play Great Britain in a Davis Cup-style challenge match prior to Wimbledon 1927, great media interest was aroused and those chosen to play were thrust into the spotlight. It was such bad luck for J. C. Gregory to be indisposed on the very eve of the match, but this gave D. M. Greig his big chance as he was called into the British team as a last-minute replacement.

Playing Bill Tilden in the opening match on Thursday 16 June was certainly a daunting prospect, but Greig approached it positively, determined not to let himself down and to make it a day to remember. It certainly proved to be that.

As Tilden arrived at the well-appointed ground of the Northern Club at West Didsbury, Manchester, a large expectant crowd awaited the contest on grass, despite the rather gloomy weather. One has to wonder whether Tilden had been told about Manchester's reputation for rain or whether he had read that morning's forecast: 'A depression is approaching our Western seaboard from the Atlantic,' it said, 'bringing cloud and then rain to the North West.' Either way, Bill Tilden certainly seemed like a man in a hurry as he opened the match.

He swept through the first set 6–0 playing what one reporter described as 'simply inspired tennis'. The second set was no different as the hapless Greig again failed to win a game. Not until he was 4–0 up in the third did Tilden let a game slip as he finally wrapped the match up 6–0, 6–0, 6–2.

So Greig had been beaten by a man who later declared that 'I have never played better.' Was it really such an oddity?

For the answer to that one we must check the clock, for the entire match had lasted only 22 minutes. That's a speed record for the shortest ever best-of-five-sets match that remains in the record books to this day.

The Times report proclaimed Tilden as 'a lawn tennis genius'. 'His drives were masterly,' they drooled, 'the speed and placing of his serve mechanically perfect, and his volleying, lobbing and smashing all betrayed the master hand.'

They continued with a game stab at damage limitation: 'Greig is one of our leading men and he played well up to his usual form but Tilden made him look a mere tyro.' If that was supposed to lift Greig's spirits it failed dismally. He lost his second singles two days later as the Americans swept the board 5–0.

Perhaps the canniest member of the British team was the man who didn't play. J. C. Gregory's indisposition never was fully explained.

Might it have been a bad attack of Tildenitis?

BIG HEAD DONISTHORPE

QUEEN'S CLUB, LONDON, OCTOBER 1927

It was in the 1920s that lawn tennis players first thought of turning 'professional', which meant exclusion from the major championships but a chance to ply their trade for legitimate money in exhibition games and on the professional tours which were beginning to develop.

One man who decided to give it a go was the English player F. W. Donisthorpe. He'd done pretty well at Wimbledon in 1919 and 1921 and certainly fancied his chances on the pro circuit.

Frank Donisthorpe duly got down to it with gusto and when the Gipsy Club in Highbury, North London, held the first open professional tournament in Britain in 1925, he beat Charles Read 6–4, 6–1, 6–4 in the final to win it.

Later that same year he had his name engraved on the official British Professional Championship Cup, although curiously he won that impressive-sounding title without playing a single match. The championship was run on a challenge basis, rather like a boxing title fight and when the ever-confident Frank had thrown down the gauntlet to the holder, the champion refused to play on the grounds that the £25 purse was insufficient.

A hollow victory? So what? It was the Lawn Tennis Association who quite ludicrously awarded him the title. Big Frank was on a roll.

Two years later, when the tennis-mad author Gilbert

Frankau suggested that his newly launched magazine *Britannia and Eve* was proposing to run a world professional championship, with a prize of £50, Frank was in like a flash.

Grandly titled as it was, this was essentially a British event because the sponsors refused to pay travel expenses for overseas players. Naturally, they nearly all refused to come.

No matter, for when the tournament began on the Queen's Club hard courts in early October 1927, Frank played out of his skin and advanced to the semi-finals.

It was a pity it rained on the Saturday of the match but just as well they were able to switch to the indoor wooden surface.

His opponent that day was 19-year-old Dan Maskell, later revered as 'the voice of tennis' but then knocking balls regularly enough over the high part of the net to be set to become a real force in the professional game.

Now everybody knows that Dan was a true gentleman, which makes it mighty strange that he was never able to write or talk about that match with Donisthorpe without working the words 'big head' somewhere into the tale.

But that's where the strangeness comes in, for Frank Donisthorpe's real claim to fame lies not in his tennis prowess but in the size of racket he used. 'The Donisthorpe' was, quite simply, enormous.

Pictures of Frank wielding the mighty beast, which took Wimbledon completely by surprise when he first used it there, show it to be much longer and about half as wide again as the standard wooden frame then in vogue and bigger, even, than today's mega-monsters favoured by club players seeking a better chance of putting string to ball.

But let's be fair to Frank. He really wasn't a big head. In fact he was one of the nicest, most modest chaps the game has seen, a character trait which gave another most curious twist to his contest with Maskell, who later recounted the yarn in his autobiography: 'We had to play the semi-finals and finals on the same day, but Charles Read got a walkover in his semi when his opponent scratched. I won my first set against Donisthorpe 6–4 and was leading 2–0 in the second when he came to the net and said "Dan, I'm going to scratch. You are going to beat me anyway so you might as well be fresh for this afternoon's final against Read, who hasn't had to play."'

Despite Maskell's predictable reply that 'You can't possibly do that,' Donisthorpe was as good as his word and Maskell later prevailed over Read to become World Professional Champion that very afternoon, courtesy of surely the most generous retirement gesture in tennis history.

Donisthorpe rarely features in tennis discussions now but back in the 1920s he was the talk of the circuit and *all* his matches were oddities.

Old 'Big Head' deserves to be remembered, though. Fully 50 years before Prince, Head, and other mega-merchants of the hi-tech equipment scene launched their own innovatory oversize products, Frank Donisthorpe had been there, done that, got the T-shirt.

JOAD'S GAMBIT

BIRKBECK COLLEGE, LONDON, JUNE 1931

Nowadays, only real head-in-the-sand types have never heard of Gamesmanship. But it wasn't always so, for the term was only conceived in June 1931, first written down in 1933 and didn't truly enter the English language until 1947.

In the true spirit of surreality, which pervades this most ingenious of tennis tactics, the match in which 'Gamesmanship' was born is an automatic choice for our collection of tennis oddities.

In truth, tennis players have been at it since time immemorial, but under the name of 'guile', 'trickery' or other such epithets. But it took the English writer, educationalist and broadcaster Stephen Potter to invent a name for it and to elevate Gamesmanship to a high art.

Stephen Meredith Potter was born in Wandsworth, London, on 12 February 1900. In his 1959 autobiography *Steps to Immaturity* he tells us he sprang from a family whose liking for games was 'fifty times stronger than their natural ability' and therein lies the genesis of his Gamesmanship. It was 'needs must'.

Described by one of his contemporaries as 'a big overgrown boy with a great deal of charm' he was educated at Westminster School and Oxford University before taking up a lecturing post at Birkbeck College in London and later joining the staff of the BBC as a writer and literary producer.

In 1947 the book which was to change his life was

published. *The Theory and Practice of Gamesmanship or The Art of Winning Games Without Actually Cheating* became an instant bestseller. Tennis features prominently and Potter himself explains how the whole phenomenon started on 8 June 1931 in the grounds of Birkbeck College when he and his lecturer colleague C. E. M. Joad, well known to a generation for his appearances on the panel of BBC Radio's 'Brains Trust', took on 'two charming, well-mannered young students' whom he calls 'Smith and Brown':

> We found ourselves opposite a couple of particularly tall and athletic young men from University College. The knock-up showed that Joad and I had no chance. They won the toss and Smith cracked down a cannonball service to Joad which moved so fast that Joad, while making some effort to suggest by his attitude that he had thought the ball was going to be a fault, nevertheless was unable to get near with his racket, which he did not even attempt to move. Service to me. Having had time to gauge the speed, the next one did, in fact, graze the edge of my racket frame. Thirty-love. Now Smith again to Joad, who this time, as the ball came straight towards him, was able, by grasping the racket firmly with both hands, to receive the ball on the strings, whereupon it shot back to the other side and volleyed into the stop-netting, without hitting the ground, fully 12 feet behind Brown.

With the score at forty–love Joad, perhaps from a sort of sub-conscious desperation, is about to invent Gamesmanship in its most primitive form which Potter, with the aid of a suitable diagram, is later to chronicle:

> Smith at S1 is about to cross over to serve to me (at P). When Smith gets to a point (K) not less than one foot and not more than two feet beyond the centre of the court, Joad, standing at J2, called across the net in an even tone: 'Kindly say clearly, please, whether the ball was in or out.' [Remember, it was at least 12 feet 'long'!]

Smith, a model of sportsmanship and behaviour, is phased.

SMITH: I'm so sorry – I *thought* it was out. What did you think, Brown?

BROWN: I *thought* it was out but do let's have it again.

JOAD: No, I don't want to have it again. I only want you to say clearly, if you will, whether the ball is in or out.

The seeds of self-doubt on which all Gamesmanship gambits are based, have been well and truly set in the young minds of Smith and Brown. Their etiquette and sportsmanship have been questioned. Thus completely unsettled, their game falls apart and the oldsters, Potter and Joad, go on to win the match.

'That night I thought long and hard,' concludes Potter. 'Could not this simple gambit of Joad's be extended to other aspects of the game?'

And indeed it was, developed to a degree of sophistication so far advanced as to make Joad's Gambit look merely prehistoric.

'Clothesmanship' was another early Joad favourite to throw an opponent off-stroke. He would turn up for an important game in a yellow shirt and sporting an orange scarf to hold up his cream trousers which were worn sufficiently half-mast to reveal jet-black socks above his off-white pumps; for a casual knockabout, meanwhile, he would, naturally, wear pristine whites. Thus completely thrown either way, his hapless opponents were sure to falter.

That is the merest tip of the iceberg, which makes Potter essential reading for all true tennis amateurs.

There is of course a delicious apocryphal tone in much of Potter's writing, but the real point of it all is to 'imagine' it's true. Which of course it is!

Potter's biographer Alan Jenkins tells us that many readers, and particularly a number of psychologists at American universities, took some of it very seriously indeed and conducted analytical studies of Potter's precepts.

Even to this day, his books are classified under psychology rather than humour in many American libraries.

Potter, who died in 1969, aged 69, would surely have been amused by that in his uniquely British way. He knew better than most that tennis can be fun!

AND THEY'RE OFF!

WIMBLEDON, JUNE 1931

'In olden days a glimpse of stocking was looked on as something shocking now heaven knows . . . anything goes.'

When Cole Porter's famous song was first introduced to Broadway audiences in November 1934 it certainly summed up the mood of the 1930s as bright young things threw caution to the wind.

Not a song about tennis fashion, but it might well have been. It would explain why an otherwise routine second round ladies' singles match at Wimbledon 1931 between Britain's Mrs Joan Lycett and the glamorous Spaniard Miss Lili de Alvarez occupies a significant place in the record books to this day.

Right from the early days of lawn tennis, the ladies' 'dress suitability' question aroused constant interest. When 15-year-old Lottie Dod won Wimbledon in 1887 wearing a calf-length skirt, the glimpse of stockinged ankle was only deemed acceptable because she was a mere girl and the dress was an integral part of her school uniform.

When the English-born, but suitably liberalized, Californian May Sutton won the 1905 Championship, Wimbledon raised an eyebrow when the hem of a fully fledged woman hovered above the ankle for the first time; and not only that . . . she revealed her bare wrists by turning up the cuffs of her long-sleeved shirt.

Then Suzanne Lenglen really broke the mould in 1919. Her

flimsy one-piece cotton frock, calf-length, short-sleeved and worn without petticoats was a real first, a classic case of French chic. Like all before her, though, she still wore stockings, although La Lenglen's habit of wearing them rolled down to the lower thigh was surely the thin edge of the wedge.

Sure enough, on the scorching hot Tuesday of 21 June 1927, Miss Ruth Tapscott stepped on to Court 10 as the first woman to appear at Wimbledon without wearing stockings. *The Times* reported that 'Run she can and run she did, stopping quickly, slithering, skidding, running all out . . . indeed running as if she liked it.' Evidently a shockingly liberal girl, but *The Times* tolerated the bare legs on account of her being 'a very young lady from South Africa'.

Only one taboo remaining. Bare legs on Centre Court. The Wimbledon committee fretted. Some brazen hussy would surely do it and offend Queen Mary. In 1929 guidelines were issued but no regulation was laid down. The assistant secretary Nora Cleather later wrote that 'the weighty matter of stocking-less legs on Centre Court shall be left to the players' own good taste'.

The bombshell came on Tuesday 23 June 1931. When officials spotted Joan Lycett about to parade her naked legs they rushed up and told her to put some stockings on. Her simple reply transcended nearly 50 years of Wimbledon ladies' history: 'But I haven't got any.'

Naturally enough the matter again made the pages of *The Times*, which described Joan Lycett as 'daring' and 'a pioneer'. Even Fleet Street's most august institution, though, reported the matter with an air of resignation and a tiny discernible twinkle in the eye. Joan Lycett was beaten by Lili de Alvarez 2–6, 6–1, 6–2 but she won the day for women's liberation.

Wimbledon was not laid to waste by an almighty strike of lightning, nor was the monarchy destroyed.

Of postscripts to this strange affair there are two. The only person really to make a spectacle of herself that Tuesday afternoon was the French player Rosie Berthet. The crowd might well have shouted 'Cor, what a pair' as she became the first player to appear on Centre Court wearing . . . glasses!

In 1933, Joan Lycett's brother H. W. 'Bunny' Austin decided to keep things in the family by staging his own revealing knees-up. On the first Thursday he became the first male player ever to wear shorts on Centre Court.

What is really strange about such incidents is that they should have been perceived as strange at all in an age when all sorts of liberal goings-on occurred behind closed doors. It was, one supposes, the overtly public airing of bare flesh, not in a bedroom, a theatre or on a beach, but at Wimbledon dammit, that caused the fuss.

Now everything's topsy turvy. Imagine if Pete Sampras sported long flannels today or Anna Kournikova flouted convention by turning out with stockings.

Something tells me the front pages might once again beckon.

A PHANTOM FINAL

WIMBLEDON, JULY 1931

It has only happened once in over 400 occasions but then 1931 Wimbledon champion Sidney Wood seemed intent on entering the record books for something right from an early age.

When he first appeared at Wimbledon as a precocious 15-year-old in 1927 he astonished the Centre Court in his first-round match against then World No. 1 René Lacoste by marching into the vast arena entirely unconcerned clad in white plus-fours and golfing stockings. He lost the match but won the hearts of the Wimbledon crowd and gave the newspaper cartoonists some ready-made material.

By 1931 his game had developed to such a degree that he was a serious challenger to anybody but, although he'd become a regular in the American Davis Cup team, he'd never won a Grand Slam singles title.

But this was to be his year and what he achieved has never been emulated in over 400 men's finals since the Wimbledon-US-French-Australian quartet of events began. Yet strangely enough it gave him no satisfaction whatsoever and what should have been a dream come true turned into a distinctly bad day for the stylish youngster from Black Rock, Connecticut. Events also sparked off some bitter feelings in the ranks of British tennis officialdom and fans alike.

Wood's great friend was his fellow Davis Cup team-mate Frank Shields, later the grandfather of the more recently

101

famous Brooke Shields, actress and former wife of André Agassi.

Seeded at No. 7 and 3 respectively the draw allowed for a possible meeting in the final. Sure enough they both battled their way through and tennis fans with finals tickets for Saturday 4 July relished the prospect of an all-American Independence Day classic.

They didn't get it. That American invention the Davis Cup saw to that. Back in 1900 they'd challenged Britain and the world to a battle for tennis supremacy but the Americans had been having a bad time of it lately. The famous Musketeers had kept the trophy in France ever since 1927 and the Americans wanted it back more than anything in tennis. Straight after Wimbledon they faced a showdown inter-zone final with Great Britain in Paris. Nothing would stand in their way of winning that one for a final place and certainly not a British crowd who'd paid good money in the foolish hope of seeing a mere Wimbledon final.

In his semi-final against legendary French Musketeer, Jean Borotra, the Bounding Basque, Frank Shields had fallen behind 2 sets to 1 and then hurt an ankle. It proved to be nothing that a 12-minute massage couldn't ease and Shields stormed back to satisfy American honour and march into the final with a victory in five sets. His friend and colleague Sidney Wood awaited.

It was then that US Davis Cup captain Gene Dixon pulled the fastest trick in tennis history. Despite winning two sets with an 'injury' against one of the best players in the world, Shields, he said, was not fit to play Woods. The ankle simply wouldn't stand it.

So the two key US Davis Cup players enjoyed a welcome rest and the Wimbledon final was cancelled.

Thus Sidney Wood became the only man in entire tennis history to have won a Grand Slam title by a walkover as the 'Phantom Final' entered the record books.

British tennis was not amused, even less so when Shields was declared fit for the Davis Cup tie and promptly beat Fred Perry 10–8, 6–4, 6–2 to help the Americans to a 2–1 lead. 'He was,' wrote a sceptical British reporter, 'obviously fit as he charged the net and lunged for volleys.'

Strangely enough in the light of more recent Davis Cup history, Britain had the last laugh. Perry beat Sidney 'Walkover' Wood to level the scores and they clinched the tie 3–2 as 'Scratcher' Shields lost to Bunny Austin in the deciding rubber. Not until 1937 would USA lift the Davis Cup again.

Fred Perry seemingly spoke for a nation when he addressed the Americans in Paris with a typically blunt little observation to another of their team, George Lott. 'Your boys seemed very over-confident,' he told the teeth-gritted loser, 'and they are really not that good, you know.'

PERRY'S REVENGE

MELBOURNE, AUSTRALIA, JANUARY 1935

Once upon a time there was a British tennis player called Fred Perry. He wasn't from a privileged background but won Wimbledon three times in a row, helped Britain to four successive Davis Cup triumphs, turned professional, became Champion of the World and made his fortune.

That might be a fairy tale by today's standards but back in the 1930s it was the story that really did make the headlines. Let it not be thought, though, that Frederick John Perry, son of a Stockport cotton-spinner, was invincible.

He did lose tennis matches and the player who came to be known as his bogeyman was the ambidextrous Italian Giorgio de Stefani, who constantly changed hands to hit every shot as a forehand. The problem with Perry, or perhaps we should say his greatest asset, was that he hated losing and, to put it bluntly, de Stefani got right up Fred's nose.

It was a rivalry which was to lead to the grudge match of all time.

Perry's losing streak started in Paris in 1931 when the Italian dumped him out of the French Championships in the last 16. It continued in a Davis Cup tie at Eastbourne's Devonshire Park in 1933 when, despite Britain beating Italy comfortably 4–1, it was Perry who lost the only rubber against you know who.

Following those two rare reversals, Perry vowed his revenge. But when they next met at the French Championships in 1934, he again lost, this time in four sets after winning the first and then injuring an ankle in the second, which he lost 6–1. Perry thought of retiring hurt but agreed with de Stefani that he would carry on provided the Italian 'took it easy' on his way to victory. Perry later wrote: 'He obviously didn't trust me because he kept me running, which made me real mad, and I lost an uncomfortable match.'

For Perry the blue touchpaper had been lit and he further wrote: 'As we came off court I said "Right Giorgio, next time we play it's going to be 6–0, 6–0, 6–0."'

It wasn't until the 1935 Australian Championships that a draw pitted them against each other again. High noon was set for the country club surroundings of Kooyong in Melbourne on Wednesday 9 January 1935, but the prospects again looked grim for Perry.

He'd already been beaten before Christmas in the Victoria State Championships and his performances in Melbourne before the quarter-final against de Stefani had been highly erratic. After his win in an early round of the mixed, *The Times* was moved to report that 'Perry played with keenness but was unsteady on the forehand, lacking his normal power and accuracy.' And after a men's doubles, 'Perry could do little right.'

The chances of his jibe to de Stefani being thrown firmly back into his face looked ominously high.

Thank goodness for strange happenings! *The Times* duly reported of the showdown that 'the return to form of F. J. Perry was almost startling, playing each stroke as if he were determined to make a winner of it'.

Almost startling? What does it take to rouse those 1930s' tennis writers? The record books say it all and confirm why Fred Perry was the winner he was.

F. J. Perry (GB) beat G. de Stefani (Italy) 6–0, 6–0, 6–0.

A LIFE-CHANGING CALL

DAVIS CUP, WIMBLEDON, JULY 1937

Players have been complaining about bad calls since the game began. Some even claim that the course of their entire careers hinged on a line judge's shout of 'Out' at a crucial moment. But for the German star Baron Gottfried Von Cramm there was one call which really did change his life, and it came from an unusual source.

The baron was one of the greatest tennis players of the 1930s and one of the most distinguished and sporting gentlemen the game has ever known. Impeccable in both dress and manners, dashingly handsome and a supremely graceful strokemaker, he captured the public's fancy wherever he played.

As Germany prepared to play USA in the inter-zone final of the Davis Cup, a nation increasingly obsessed with their ambitions for world domination expected much. A challenge-round final against holders Great Britain awaited the victors.

Baron Gottfried Alexander Maximilian Walter Kurt Von Cramm was as fervently patriotic as his noble lineage would suggest but didn't always see eye to eye with the current political regime. When his Jewish team-mate Daniel Prenn was banished from the Davis Cup team, the baron openly criticized the Nazi party and persistently refused to join their ranks despite repeated invitations from Field Marshal Hermann Goering to do so.

He had already irritated German image-builders in a 1935

Davis Cup defeat against USA when, despite the umpire's call of 'game, set and match Germany', he admitted to having faintly touched a ball when no one else had noticed. The point was given to USA and his sportsmanship ultimately cost Germany the tie.

Although fiercely criticized in the German camp for this 'traitorous act', he remained beyond ultimate censure so long as he held the capacity to enhance the status of the Fatherland. The year 1937, surely, was a second chance for Germany to win their first Davis Cup and for the dashing baron to be their hero.

On day one Von Cramm defeated Brian 'Bitsy' Grant in his first singles. America's star Donald Budge levelled the tie by taking his singles. On day two Von Cramm lost with his partner Henkel in the doubles and by the final day the tie stood at 2–2.

All now depended on the final singles between Von Cramm and Budge.

As they walked on to Wimbledon's Centre Court on 20 July the atmosphere was electric. In the 14,000 crowd were Queen Mary, German ambassador to Great Britain Joachim von Ribbentrop, the German minister for sport and a host of American officials and fans.

But Germany's most nationalistic supporter, Adolf Hitler, was otherwise engaged. Not so his telephone, though. As the players approached the court, a locker-room boy intercepted to say Von Cramm was wanted on the telephone, long distance. It was to be the most significant 'call' of his life.

Donald Budge always insisted he distinctly heard Von Cramm say, *'Ja, mein Führer'* several times. Von Cramm was later to deny this, but tennis history now accepts that the 'good luck' call *was* from Hitler himself.

'You *will* win' was the gist of the message. Germany's star walked on court looking strangely pale and serious as the swastika flag fluttered ominously over SW19.

Von Cramm won the first two sets 7–5, 8–6. Budge took the third 6–4 and the fourth 6–2. In the decisive fifth, the baron looked poised for victory at 4–1 but Budge clawed back to 4–4 as the tension mounted.

Allison Danzig of the *New York Times* was later to write: 'The brilliance of the tennis was almost unbelievable as the gallery looked on spellbound and two great players worked miracles of redemption and riposte in rallies of breakneck pace ranging all over the court in a cascade of electrifying strokes.'

He was writing of an American victory. Despite saving four match points Von Cramm finally succumbed 8–6 as Budge hit a diving final winner at 8.45 pm in semi-darkness. Having just lost the most important match of his life the response of the baron was typical of his character.

Smilingly approaching the net he shook hands:

'Don,' he said, 'this was absolutely the finest match I have ever played in my life. I'm very happy that I could have played it against you, whom I like so very much. Congratulations.'

But the Führer had little use for a gracious loser. After further Von Cramm criticisms of the Nazi regime filtered back to Hitler's all-hearing ears, retribution quickly followed.

On 5 July 1938 two Gestapo agents called on Von Cramm at his family castle in Bruggen and he was taken to a Berlin prison and charged with 'sex irregularities', namely having had a homosexual affair with Manasse Herbst, a German-Jewish actor. It was true, and in those undoubtedly licentious but still unenlightened days a perfect pretext on which to imprison the guilty party.

He served five months before gaining refuge in Sweden. A loyal German to the end he fought as a gunner during the war in the Russian campaign of 1942, suffered frostbite in both legs and was awarded the Iron Cross. Then, in yet another bizarre twist, he was promptly dishonourably discharged from the army on suspicion of plotting against Hitler's life.

Although he played tennis again, appearing at Wimbledon one last time in 1951, he never achieved his ambition of winning that tournament or the Davis Cup and his turbulent and remarkable life ended on 9 November 1976 in Egypt, when the car he was being driven in was hit by a military truck.

When Boris Becker won his first Wimbledon in 1985 he announced that his victory would give the sport a much-needed boost in his country because 'in Germany we never had an idol before in tennis'.

Boris was the youngest-ever Wimbledon men's champion, just 17 years 227 days, so might be forgiven his *faux pas*. His victory came on 7 July 1985. It would have been Von Cramm's seventy-sixth birthday. Perhaps the new German idol hadn't heard of the man who was called 'out' by Hitler so many years before.

A MOST EMPHATIC COMEBACK

BOURNEMOUTH, APRIL 1938

When Kho Sin Kie and Mr W. C. Choy arrived at the West Hants Club, Bournemouth, in the spring of 1938 for the Hard Court Championships of Great Britain they carried the hopes of Chinese tennis with them.

Few top-quality players had emerged from their millions but having joined the International Lawn Tennis Federation earlier in the year the nation hoped to turn the tide.

No Chinese player had ever won an official Federation tournament. Kho Sin Kie had taken the Greek Championship and caused a stir in Alexandria, Egypt, but his form on the Continent was erratic and he was unseeded by the Bournemouth committee.

Nor was Choy regarded as much more than curiosity value in an era when patronizing phrases such as 'the little Chinese' and 'the men from the East' still stood out in tennis press coverage.

The field was strong. Britain's H. W. 'Bunny' Austin was first seed and future Wimbledon champion, the Frenchman Yvon Petra, was well fancied.

But the Chinese started well, both progressing to the quarter-finals where they met each other. Kho Sin Kie, in particular, had paid scant regard to the old-guard traditions of British tennis, hammering the makeweight Lord Pollington in the first round and reaching the quarters without loss of a set. Meanwhile, when Austin beat Petra *Lawn Tennis* magazine described the match as 'the virtual final'.

All seemed set for a continuance of British domination although one or two Bournemouth sages were heard to mutter that Kie might be a threat.

The Chinese twosome faced each other on Thursday 28 April in one of the most remarkable matches in tennis history. All seemed up for Kie as Choy played out of his skin to take the first two sets 6–4, 6–4.

When Choy went 1–0 up in the third the road back for Kie seemed unlikely and 'Bunny' Austin fans began counting their chickens.

No one knows quite what came over Kie at that point but his stroke selection was evidently judicious as 'he drop shotted his opponent groggy'.

Choy didn't slack off. He was simply outwitted by 'the crafty Oriental' in the most emphatic comeback of all time as Kie won 18 successive games to take the last three sets 6–1, 6–0, 6–0.

Maybe it was the Year of the Tiger. Kie certainly played like one as he then stormed through the semis to shock Austin in the final with a victory in four sets in front of 4,000 bemused spectators.

The report from 'The Man on the Line' in *Lawn Tennis* magazine struck an astonished stance:

> Kho Sin Kie's final victory was little short of a triumph in the unenviable conditions as a strong and gusty cross wind and eddies of red sand swirled round the court, sometimes stopping play. He seemed completely unaffected, working up for his coups with the foresight of a chess grand master, overcoming the pranks of the wind by magnificent ball control in a triumph of modern science over a veteran academic as Austin finally surrendered with a rather exhausted double fault.

He was both the first Chinese and the only unseeded player ever to have taken a British national singles title and the country that invented lawn tennis was rather shocked.

111

The *Lawn Tennis* correspondent voiced the fears of a nation: 'Is the writing on the wall? World form is evidently levelling up with the increasing spread of the game and the Chinese ace's convincing Bournemouth win may foreshadow the time when other major championships will be captured by representatives of the younger tennis nations.'

Never was an observation truer. Kho Sin Kie's victory via his amazing quarter-final comeback was a symbolic turning point for our domestic game.

The 'younger tennis nations' did indeed come of age. Not since Fred Perry's victory in 1936 has a British man won Wimbledon.

PLAY WILL CONTINUE

SHIRLEY PARK, CROYDON, SEPTEMBER 1939

Miss Vera Dace of the Denmark Hill Lawn Tennis Club hoped for the best when she entered the Surrey summer singles competition played on the red clay of the Shirley Park Lawn Tennis Club in Croydon.

She didn't expect to win but as an up-and-coming prospect in the ladies' game she intended to turn a few heads.

And that she did, reaching the final in fine style. The September weather, though, hadn't been entirely kind to the organizers and the lady finalists had to convene on the Sunday morning, the day after the tournament had been scheduled to finish. It was a quirk of timing that was to give Vera Dace a unique place in lawn tennis history.

Never has a date been more significant. It was 3 September 1939 and, as Vera fought for victory, there was another battle of wits, altogether more crucial, going on elsewhere.

When King George VI had appealed the night before for the need to 'stand calm, firm and united' it wasn't an exhortation to young Vera to keep her focus on the game ahead but a heartfelt plea to the people of a nation on the brink of war.

Everybody knew it was coming. All the preparations were in place. Only the timing remained to be decided. As Vera Dace prepared for her match that Sunday morning the British ambassador in Berlin was handing the German government an official note stating that unless they confirmed their willingness by 11 am to withdraw their troops from Poland a state of

113

war would exist between England and Germany.

Time ticked away as Vera's match progressed. At 11.15 the prime minister, Neville Chamberlain, broadcast to a waiting nation possibly the most famous words ever to be carried on the airwaves: 'I have to tell you that no such undertaking has been received and that consequently this country is at war with Germany.'

Vera was just one game from clinching victory as the sirens sounded to signal the outbreak of war. It was a trial run of sorts and everybody had been instructed to head for the shelters when the alarm sounded.

But being a sensible sort of fellow the umpire at Shirley Park figured that the chance of German planes bombarding Croydon that morning was remote, to say the least.

'Play will continue,' he asserted. *Lawn Tennis* magazine later confirmed the happy outcome: 'Miss Dace wanted only one game for victory when the first siren sounded, but play continued until the match was won and lost. A cup was thrust into her hands by a county official and all concerned took a dive into the nearest air-raid shelter.'

So much would happen during the war that followed, but many tennis clubs would try to emulate the Dace spirit by carrying on. Some, like the members at the Hollies Club in Wilford, Nottinghamshire, would be scuppered by matters outside their control. They arrived at the club one day to find a Flying Fortress bomber embedded in their courts!

But others would play on and Britain, like Vera Dace, would come through for victory. People may not remember her now but she remains the only player in the lawn tennis record books to have started a final in peacetime and won it during wartime.

FANTASY TENNIS

ALDERSHOT, FEBRUARY 1941

That a single tennis match should be read about by someone, somewhere, every single day, over 60 years later, is perhaps not so strange. Truly great matches are, after all, still being well aired.

That the contest was between a man and a woman and that neither player was from the top drawer suggests something a little more curious. But what really qualifies this immortal game for entry into the gallery of strangeness is that it never took place at all. It was 'fantasy tennis' of the highest order.

Perhaps it has something to do with the virginal white attire, tanned athletic limbs, grace of movement or the relentless summer sun, but there is something about an idealized vision of tennis which inspires daydreaming. Who hasn't pondered the sublime promise of a set with Gabriella Sabatini or Anna Kournikova? Or a practice session with Bjorn Borg or Greg Rusedski? My choices are random, for there are countless others; irrespective of gender or age preference we all have our favourites.

In reality these things do not happen, nor are they written about or recalled. Unless, that is, one happens to be one of the most celebrated poets of the twentieth century.

John Betjeman's poem 'A Subaltern's Love Song' first appeared in print in *Horizon* in February 1941 and has subsequently been reprinted in anthologies the world over. It relates a match between Betjeman, in the guise of a young second lieutenant, and the object of his desire, Miss Joan Hunter Dunn:

Miss J. Hunter Dunn, Miss J. Hunter Dunn,
Furnish'd and burnish'd by Aldershot sun,
What strenuous singles we played after tea,
We in the tournament – you against me!

Love-thirty, love-forty, oh! weakness of joy,
The speed of a swallow, the grace of a boy,
With carefullest carelessness, gaily you won,   ⌡
I am weak from your loveliness, Joan Hunter Dunn.

Miss Joan Hunter Dunn, Miss Joan Hunter Dunn,
How mad I am, sad I am, glad that you won.
The warm-handled racket is back in its press,
But my shock-headed victor, she loves me no less.

Her father's euonymus shines as we walk,
And swing past the summer house, buried in talk,
And cool the verandah that welcomes us in
To the six o'clock news and a lime-juice and gin.

The scent of the conifers, sound of the bath,
The view from my bedroom of moss-dappled path,
As I struggle with double-end evening tie,
For we dance at the Golf Club, my victor and I.

On the floor of her bedroom lie blazer and shorts
And the cream-coloured walls are betrophied with sports,
And westering, questioning settles the sun
On your low-leaded window, Miss Joan Hunter Dunn.

The Hillman is waiting, the light's in the hall,
The pictures of Egypt are bright on the wall,
My sweet, I am standing beside the oak stair
And there on the landing's the light on your hair.

By roads 'not adopted', by woodlanded ways,
She drove to the club in the late-summer haze,
Into nine o'clock Camberley, heavy with bells
And mushroomy, pine-woody, evergreen smells.

Miss Joan Hunter Dunn, Miss Joan Hunter Dunn,
I can hear from the car-park the dance has begun.
Oh! full Surrey twilight! importunate band!
Oh! strongly adorable tennis-girl's hand!

Around us are Rovers and Austins afar,
Above us the intimate roof of the car,
And here on my right is the girl of my choice,
With the tilt of her nose and the chime of her voice.

And the scent of her wrap, and the words never said,
And the ominous, ominous dancing ahead.
We sat in the car-park till twenty to one
And now I'm engaged to Miss Joan Hunter Dunn.

Quite some way from a Grand Slam event but it is tennis and romance as many have recognized it and still like to imagine it.

The game never occurred, nor was there an engagement, but, contrary to what many Betjeman admirers have assumed, Miss Joan Hunter Dunn was, as the future Poet Laureate explained 21 years later, real flesh and blood:

> At the start of the war I was employed in the films division of the Ministry of Information and Joan was employed by London University in the same building as second in command of the catering department. She wore a white coat and had a clean, clinical, motherly look which excited hundreds of us. She had bright cheeks, clear sun-burned skin, darting brown eyes, a shock of dark curls and a happy smile and her figure was a dream of strength and beauty. I wrote the verses in the character of a subaltern in Aldershot but they were really my own imaginings about her. Actually she was from Farnborough. Oh goodness, I wish you had seen her striding about the ministry.

When Joan married in 1945, John was invited but conveniently 'unable to attend'.

Sir John Betjeman (1906–84) died on 19 May 1984, aged

117

77, frail and wheelchair-bound from the ravages of Parkinson's disease, yet each day a Betjeman admirer somewhere causes the clock to be wound back to wartime Aldershot and the unblemished abandon of relative youth.

And so this famous match, at once the purest and yet most erotic of all tennis encounters, is perpetually replayed.

Betjeman has achieved lasting fame as a poet and Joan Hunter Dunn, without ever hitting a ball in serious competition, has achieved immortality in the annals of lawn tennis.

MANY HAPPY RETURNS

SUTTON, SURREY, APRIL 1946

The Surrey Open Hard Court Championships of 1946 were
something of a celebration for British tennis as a jubilant
nation looked forward to its first full summer season after the
end of war. The Surrey Tournament was the first post-war
Open of the new era and *Lawn Tennis and Badminton*
magazine set the scene admirably:

> Exceptionally large crowds attracted by the galaxy of talent
> and the glorious spring weather flocked to the Sutton club.
> The grounds are well appointed and no longer bear any trace
> of the London blitz although a stick of bombs fell on the
> clubhouse in 1940 and a blitzed house within 20 yards of the
> centre court serves as a reminder of ordeals now past.

The players were as eager as the public to embrace the
'business as usual' spirit and entries came from far and wide,
none more so than that of Australia's Jack Harper, only
recently arrived from down under for the European season.

And for him, ranked 8 in his home country and seeded 2 at
Surrey, the second day of the tournament offered the opportunity for a remarkable personal celebration never likely to be
repeated.

Tuesday 9 April was Jack Harper's thirty-second birthday.
Drawn to play the British player J. Sandiford in a three-set
contest, Harper might well have contemplated the pleasure of

119

a birthday victory but surely nothing could have prepared him or the Sutton gallery for what actually happened.

Maybe the Aussie had a party and a few beers lined up, because he certainly seemed in a hurry. The short, sharp match report is a perfect summary of the game itself: 'The match lasted only 18 minutes as Harper won 6–0, 6–0 for the loss of only one point.'

It was a pity for Sandiford that breaks between change of ends hadn't then been introduced. At least nowadays he'd have lasted nearly half an hour, had a swig of Coke and buried his head in his towel. No such comforts in 1946.

Bizarrely enough this brief encounter wasn't the shortest authenticated match on record. On 13 June 1914, in the Kent Championships at Beckenham, it was again an antipodean whirlwind that hit the courts in a hurry. On that occasion Australia's Norman Brookes teamed up with legendary New Zealander Anthony Wilding to beat the experienced but flagging British pair Arthur Gore and Herbert Roper Barrett 6–2, 6–1 in just 16 minutes.

Nor is Harper's miserly restriction of his unfortunate opponent to just one point the most humiliating thrashing of all time.

In Seattle in 1910 the all-conquering Hazel Hotchkiss of the USA, now better remembered as Mrs G. W. Wightman, founder of the Wightman Cup, achieved a complete 6–0, 6–0 whitewash over her opponent Miss Huiskamp by winning 48 straight points in a row.

Another American, Pauline Betz, did the same in the Pennsylvania Tri-State tournament of 1943, this time leaving Miss C. Wolf to ruefully reflect what a 'pointless' game tennis could be.

In the men's game, though, Jack Harper is still believed to be the most emphatic winner of all time.

There is no record of how he spent his birthday night but any over-indulgence clearly had no lasting effect. He took the singles and men's doubles titles without much ado.

As for the unfortunate Sandiford, he might well have blamed his painful defeat on a bad draw but there would be plenty of other 'draw' opportunities for him to extract painful revenge from others.

Tennis for him was just a little light relief from the rigours of being a dental student.

REDL'S SPECIAL SERVICE

WIMBLEDON, JUNE 1947

'The nets are not so high as they used to be. Perhaps the players are not so good as they were before the war.' That precious little *faux pas* from a spectator at the 1946 Wimbledon was recalled with amusement by Norah Cleather in her book *Wimbledon Story*.

As acting secretary of the club during the tumultuous war years she'd seen some odd things but altering the rules of tennis to help the war-weary wasn't on the agenda.

Getting back to normal was what Wimbledon really wanted. Sixteen German bombs fell on the grounds during the conflict, including a direct hit on Centre Court. Car parks had been ploughed up to grow vegetables or house pigs, geese, chickens and rabbits.

Meanwhile the Home Guard and two regiments used the concourse as a parade ground and many of the buildings were requisitioned.

That was why it was such a relief to get through Wimbledon 1946, the first since 1939. But in many ways it was a practice run, as there were still plenty of signs of the havoc that had been caused. The real 'Wimbledon as usual' would need to wait for 1947.

But, when it came, tennis fans were treated to a curious sight. What's more, the officials had to accommodate a change to the rules to help a little Austrian who'd had a bad war. Mercifully he wasn't the same one who'd bashed a hole in the Centre Court roof.

Hans Redl had played Davis Cup for his native Austria in 1937 but after being 'persuaded' to change his nationality he played for Germany in 1938 and 1939. No one took too much notice of his first match on Court 7, but the number proved lucky as he readily disposed of a Brit.

Putting him on Court 13 in the next round made no difference as this time he rolled over a Swiss without too much bother.

By the time he'd put paid to another British hope everyone was talking about Hans Redl. *The Times* correspondent was particularly impressed by 'his fine service' and wrote admiringly of his 'gallantry'.

As all eyes focused on Redl during his last 16 clash on Court 2 on Saturday 28 June, his eighth-seeded American opponent Bob Falkenburg must have thought that the traditional support for the underdog had gone too far. But British crowds have always loved a battler and there was none more plucky than Redl.

On active service during the Battle of Stalingrad he had lost his left arm but never thought of giving up tennis. Instead he'd lobbied the ruling bodies to change the service rules, which they duly did. Redl soon mastered the art of resting the ball on his racket, flipping it into the air and thundering down his serves. The art of balance, too, was something he had to learn afresh.

Although Falkenburg won the match 6–3, 6–3, 6–4 the likeable Hans Redl was embraced by Wimbledon. He seemed, after all, to sum up the spirit of the times. Many things had changed in the wartime hiatus but now it was business as usual.

Lawn tennis and Redl had both been permanently altered by the experience but both had mercifully survived.

STURGESS HOLDS COURT

BOURNEMOUTH, MAY 1948

'Those in search of peace and tranquility need look no further than the charming seaside town of Bournemouth, a queen of resorts.'

Perhaps Eric William Sturgess had read that enticing description in his guide book *Bournemouth and its Environs*, for the 27-year-old South African had troubled to journey a long way from his Johannesburg birthplace late in April 1948 as he breathed the spring air of that regal south-coast resort.

He was, though, blissfully unaware that he was about to become its king, and that 'peace and tranquility' were certainly not in his schedule.

The West Hants Lawn Tennis Club at Melville Park had been staging the Hard Court Championships of Great Britain since 1927. As befitted a coastal town, they ran a tight ship and prided themselves on finishing on time whatever the vagaries of the British weather.

They had a good entry in 1948 and were particularly delighted to welcome back Wimbledon competitor E. W. Sturgess, who had won the triple crown at Bournemouth the previous year by taking all three titles.

When the tournament commenced on 26 April Sturgess was keen to defend his titles and, according to *Lawn Tennis* magazine, started well as 'the Championships got going to an idyllic couple of days which left the impression that fortune was at last smiling on Melville Park'.

124

They waxed positively lyrical, too, about Sturgess's game: 'His greatest assets are his wiry physique and mobility, his long stride enabling him to cover the court at great speed. He refuses to retreat beyond the baseline, adroitly half-volleying from either wing in the manner of Fred Perry. Once at the net he is rarely dislodged and has a deadly smash.'

Sturgess didn't let his admirers down, dispatching Berkshire hopeful S. Konig 6–2, 6–0, 6–0 on opening day and dropping only 11 points in the last two sets. Two more Brits quickly bit the red dust before Sturgess overcame the Pole, Spychala, in the semi-finals, again in straight sets.

Teaming up with the Dutchman van Meegeren in the men's and coaxing Miss Quertier through the mixed, Sturgess reached the semi-finals in both doubles competitions, scheduled for Friday 30 April.

As Friday dawned the tournament referee might well have been fretting about how to schedule Sturgess but by the time darkness fell he was faced with an almost certain late finish to the championships. The British weather had intervened, 'a boisterous wind and squally showers' putting paid to both semis.

The following day, Saturday 1 May, was to be one Sturgess would never forget.

A singles final and two doubles semis beckoned, possibly two doubles finals as well. Morning rain didn't bode well but the clouds cleared for a fine afternoon although the courts remained damp and slow. Long rallies were on the cards.

Sturgess started by coming through the men's doubles semi in a marathon five-setter, then stayed on court without rest to win his singles final in straight sets against Poland's Tloczynski.

Again he stayed on court to take the men's double crown, blessedly in straight sets. They say there is no rest for the wicked, nor apparently for talented South African tennis players. As far as the organizers were concerned it was straight on with the mixed semi and Sturgess and partner duly breezed into the final.

Although the referee then half-heartedly offered Sturgess

the chance to come back on the Sunday, he manfully declined the offer and clinched the mixed 6–2, 7–5 to retain his triple crown.

In one afternoon Sturgess had played 126 games and 15 sets. *Lawn Tennis* magazine was impressed: 'It was a remarkable feat of endurance; without fuss or flurry Sturgess set out to liquidate his opponents and left us in no doubt that he is a force in the world class.'

What price today's players beating the Sturgess record?

A FRILL A MINUTE

WIMBLEDON, JUNE 1949

Gertrude Augusta Moran was a good tennis player but not a
great one. Although ranked as high as fourth in the United
States, the girl from Santa Monica, California, never won any
of the Grand Slam titles yet she did win herself a permanent
place in tennis history.

Just one word supplies the reason. Knickers!

Tennis has always been preoccupied with fashion and
nowhere more so than at Wimbledon, that most proper of
tournaments where anything considered the least 'improper'
seems to take on exaggerated significance.

Ladies' shorts in the 1930s had created a tennis stir, but also
a backlash in the fashion industry. 'Too manly,' said the
critics, 'Give us feminine dresses with pastel trimmings.'

Famous tennis couturier Teddy Tinling rallied to the cause,
experimenting with colour during the otherwise drab war
years, and found himself on a roll as Wimbledon 1949 loomed.
Wimbledon responded by slapping an all-white rule on
players' attire.

'Gorgeous Gussy' Moran, as the strikingly glamorous
subject of this strange series of matches was known, had
meanwhile arrived in England unaware of the impending
clampdown and with firm instructions for Tinling: 'I'm
strictly feminine and colour is the essence of my life,' she
announced. 'I seldom play without something bright in my
hair, around my waist or even on my feet.'

Time for a touch of Tinling magic. An all-white compromise that would still keep Gussy happy. He did it with a short dress in an experimental soft rayon fabric.

'But what do I wear underneath?' asked Gussy.

Tinling responded with an improvised undergarment trimmed with no more than an inch of decorative lace. Thus were born Gussy's infamous 'lace panties'.

This completely innovatory outfit was unveiled at the pre-Wimbledon reception at Hurlingham and, to put it mildly, the pressmen and photographers went wild.

From the opening day at Wimbledon Gussy's playing schedule became the focus of massively heightened interest and 'the panties' themselves became a sort of frivolous metaphor for the official ending of wartime austerity and Wimbledon pomposity.

Would she or wouldn't she wear them? Everybody asked the same question. For the first time in history red-blooded males were heard to shout 'Keep 'em on' while Wimbledon committee men, also for the first time in history, were urging 'Get 'em off!', at least in a manner of speaking.

Gussy dithered. The *Daily Mail* telephoned Tinling with the latest from the press: 'Have you heard that hourly bulletins on the wearing of the panties are being posted in the press room?' they asked.

Tuesday 21 June. Gussy's first match, against Bea Walter. A packed expectant crowd and photo corps. Gussy bottled it and wore a trim pair of shorts. She won the match 3–6, 6–2, 6–3 and the press redoubled the frenzy to fever pitch. 'She's playing with us,' they screamed.

Wednesday 22 June, No. 1 Court against Betty Wilford. Gussy was later to confess that the undies were on, off and on again before she finally took a deep breath and went for it. She won the match 6–1, 6–4, the crowd went wild and cameraman Bob Ryder of Associated Press later won the Photographer of the Year award for his afternoon's work.

In the next few days Gussy was called upon to visit hospitals, open fêtes, give her name to a racehorse and an aircraft, and appear on stage in the West End with the Marx Brothers.

The singles run came to an end against Britain's diminutive Gem Hoahing on Centre Court. Gussy lost 6–2, 5–7, 6–3 and, in deference to the sacred arena, the panties stayed in the dressing room as the shorts made a comeback. It still didn't stop sales of Kodak films reaching an all-time high.

The panties, though, were neither out nor down, as Miss Moran progressed to the ladies' doubles final with her partner Pat Todd against fellow American pairing Louise Brough and Margaret du Pont, again scheduled for Centre Court in the presence of Queen Mary.

Once more it was 'will she or won't she?' in the press. As Wimbledon officials asserted that 'Queen Mary might not like it,' Gussy contemplated a final fling but stayed in her hotel until the last minute pondering her decision.

She telephoned Wimbledon four times before being told finally that Her Majesty, then 84, had decided not to attend on account of the heat.

And so the most famous pair of knickers in tennis history did make that Centre Court appearance. Miss Moran and Mrs Todd lost 8–6, 7–5 as the world's press got their final story.

Teddy Tinling, who for years had helped run Wimbledon as an assistant in the referee's office, severed his connection with the club when chairman Sir Louis Greig publicly thundered at an official post-tournament function that he would 'never allow Wimbledon to become a stage for designer's stunts'.

It is of course a ludicrous affair by present standards but equally an indication of how, then as now, titillation turned heads and sold newspapers.

At least Gussy was a little more coy about her undergarments than another American, Pat Stewart. At Wimbledon 1961, evidently feeling short of company, she played her second and third round matches against Suzanne Chatrier and Margaret Smith with her telephone number embroidered across her knickers.

And talking of Mrs Smith, who became Mrs court in 1967, it was 'Big Marge' who suffered the ultimate Centre Court indignity in 1975 when all the fastenings on her dress opted to come undone at the precise same moment as her knicker elastic gave way. Only a WRAF stewardess and a handful of safety pins saved her blushes.

As strange matches of 'the tennis underworld, go, though, it's those involving Gussy's gusset which are up there with the best.

In today's vernacular there's only one word for this story . . . pants!

TAPPY'S ROUTINE FINAL

FOREST HILLS, NEW YORK, SEPTEMBER 1950

Let's start with some good solid easy-to-grasp facts before getting on to the really weird stuff.

Arthur David Larsen was born in San Leandro, California, on 6 April 1925. His finest hours came 25 years later on Tuesday 5 September 1950 at Forest Hills when he beat fellow American Herbie Flam to win the US Championships for his first and only time.

It was a five-set match, Larsen winning 6–3, 4–6, 5–7, 6–4, 6–3, which features in the record books only routinely and as one of the more instantly forgettable of US finals.

The match was only strange for one reason. Art Larsen was playing in it. Indeed every match Larsen ever appeared in departed from the norm in some way and that was because Art Larsen was, on the sworn testimony of many of his contemporaries, the 'strangest tennis player of all time'.

The great Australian Ken Rosewall, never one for sensationalism, kept his observations low key: 'He was a left-hander, had a kind of happy, vague expression on his face, blond curly hair and a slim, almost delicate-looking, body, but he had a shrewd, deceptive game,' he once wrote of him. Then he added, quite simply: 'He was a very unusual character.'

Slightly more revealing was the South African Gordon Forbes, who sometimes partnered Larsen in men's doubles: 'He had uncanny ability, a rare gift of perfect touch, an inner knowledge of what was going on between the strings of the

131

racket and the surface of the ball,' he wrote, before again adding with just a touch of mystery: 'But Larsen's tennis was not the most extraordinary part of him.'

Forbes then gives just a hint of Larsen's unusual approach to the game: 'He never trained, seldom practised, smoked a lot, drank beer, sat in damp clothes and cold winds after matches, stopped up all night, slept in the dressing room, and seemed to have great difficulty changing into his tennis gear without getting stuck in his shorts or sweater.'

OK, so we have a sort of cross between a mercurial tennis genius on court, and a hell-raising playboy cum accident-prone absent-minded professor off it. Interesting, true, but surely there must be more; we need less coy witnesses.

Enter Abe Segal, a voluble South African who often travelled with Larsen and saw many of his matches: 'Believe me, there's a big difference between being weird and crazy and this Larsen is definitely crazy,' he observed early in their acquaintance.

So what else is there? It's Larsen's nickname 'Tappy' that provides the clue, for it was his patterns of on-court behaviour that really made him unique. He had what psychiatrists might today describe as a compulsive repetitive behaviour syndrome.

It was quite normal for Larsen to tap the baseline a certain number of times before receiving serve, every serve, equally commonplace if he was on 'an umpire day' for him to do the same to the match official when changing ends, or just as likely that he would tap the net or his foot depending on what he decided was his lucky routine for the day.

Nor was it that simple. Each day he would designate a lucky number, it might be 3, which would set the number of taps he needed to do each time while he was out on court. Or the number of times he would need to put on and take off his socks before even getting to court. It was, one supposes, superstition gone rather too far – but there's more.

Sometimes he would have to avoid walking on the lines between points, but then again on other days he would have to walk on them. At end changes it was sometimes essential that he walked round on the opposite side of the court to his opponent, and on other occasions that he must touch his opponent as he passed.

And then there was looking away until the last moment before receiving serve and insisting on using the same ball when he'd just won a good point, not to mention talking at intervals to the imaginary eagle which perched once in a while on his shoulder. When it alighted it would only fly off if he held the sleeve of his shirt in his teeth while waiting to receive, so that was another eccentricity that made Larsen seemingly as much 'tapped' as 'tappy'.

Need more convincing? Talking to the crowd during rallies was an entertaining foible, calling out his shot selections before he'd played them was another, and playing alternate drop-shots and lobs to make his opponent look silly was also a favourite. No wonder his South American fans called him 'El Pájaro Loco', the 'Crazy Woodpecker'.

It was, undoubtedly, a combination of pure showmanship, healthy eccentricity and genuine neurotic disorder that made Larsen the way he was but the public and players loved him for it all the same. He was one of the most popular men on the circuit, playing a sort of unworldly, stream-of-consciousness game which was a joy to behold.

Someone once asked Larsen 'why?' and surprisingly he had a logical answer:

I was quite normal until the age of 17, then I joined the Army. One day in a raid during the war, so many of my friends were killed all around me that it was a miracle I survived, so I figured I must have done something that day to bring me luck. Then it started. I went back over everything I'd done that day and followed my lucky routine for the rest of the war. Then, having survived, I took my superstitions with me into tennis and the whole thing snowballed into an obsession. The trouble is that I have so many superstitions now I sometimes forget them and that worries me even more.

So there it is. All a question of fate.

Maybe Larsen really did have a point. Who knows what the lucky number was one day in 1957, but it was the day Art Larsen, aged only 32, suffered serious head injuries in a motorcycle accident and never played tournament tennis again.

They might have called him 'crazy', 'unique', 'weird' or 'uncanny' but the tennis community was unanimous in their opinion that they rather liked Art Larsen and that the game would never be the same without 'Tappy'.

PLAYING FOR HIS LIFE

FOREST HILLS, NEW YORK, SEPTEMBER 1951

When a commentator says 'He's playing for his life' we know he doesn't mean it literally. But that was exactly what leading American amateur Guy Haines *was* doing when he faced fellow American Fred Reynolds on the grass at Forest Hills in the 1951 US Championships.

Fifth-seeded Haines was certainly expected to win the match but he set himself the task of doing it in straight sets to save himself from execution for the murder of his wife. If it all sounds rather far-fetched and the names totally unfamiliar, that's no surprise. As true tennis aficionados will already have divined we're talking films here, a medium through which even the strangest matches can be brought off merely at the whim of an imaginative director.

Alfred Hitchcock's highly acclaimed *Strangers on a Train* starts with tennis star Guy Haines making chance acquaintance with the psychotic mummy's boy Bruno Anthony on a train journey. Haines is romancing senator's daughter Ann Morton but his flirtatious wife Miriam is in the way of both the relationship and the guaranteed political career for Haines which will inevitably follow.

The creepy Bruno 'jokingly' suggests he will kill Guy's wife for him if he in turn will bump off Bruno's overbearing father. Guy 'jokingly' agrees, only to find that Bruno carries out his part of the bargain at a pleasure ground island in Metcalfe.

135

Bruno, meanwhile, has chillingly gained possession of Guy's cigarette lighter which, after Guy refuses to carry out his part of the spurious pact, he plans to plant at the scene of the crime to implicate the tennis star as a murderer. The death penalty would swiftly follow.

As Bruno embarks on the journey to the pleasure ground, Guy is being called on to court at Forest Hills. It seems only a quick three-set victory will enable Guy to intercept Bruno in time to expose the plan, clear his name, save his life and get the girl and lucrative career. Never have the stakes in a single match been higher!

Haines, normally such a methodical cat-and-mouse style of player, throws caution to the wind and plays an all-or-nothing game which astonishes the crowd and radio commentator alike. The match starts at 4.15 in glorious sunshine and Haines storms to a two-set lead before going 1–0 up in the third. All seems well.

But Reynolds hasn't read the script. He comes back to take the third as the clock showd 5.25. As the action cuts back and forth between the progress of the match and that of Bruno's journey the tension mounts.

When Bruno is jostled and drops the lighter down a grating the delay while he retrieves it offers Guy a lifeline.

The fourth set drags on to 10–all and Guy eventually takes it 12–10 to clinch the match.

Rushing straight off court (with not a bead of sweat in sight) into a waiting taxi he reaches the fairground followed all the way by his police shadows and confronts Bruno. The memorable climax sees Bruno killed on a merry-go-round spinning wildly out of control, his hand opening to reveal the unplanted lighter still in his possession. The tennis star is saved!

Unusual as the match undoubtedly is, it is made even more so by the unique opportunities offered by the medium of celluloid. Hitchcock may be universally acclaimed as a director but there was certainly a hitch in the continuity department on this one.

The match starts with the actors on a small mock-up court

136

with no tramlines then frequently cuts to long-distance real action on the vast arena of the Forest Hills stadium court. The tramlines appear and disappear with startling regularity and the court changes size time and again before our very eyes. To top it all Hitchcock exercises the director's privilege to rewrite the lawn tennis rule book as a blatant net-cord serve from Haines is judged perfectly legal.

Welcome to the wonderful world of cinema where Hitchcockian tennis is like nothing you've seen before.

A PREMATURE END

FORO ITALICO, ROME, MAY 1955

Giuseppe Merlo was no different in his ambitions from any other Italian player. Winning the Italian Championships at the famous Foro Italico in Rome would be everything he had ever dreamed of.

And now, Tuesday 10 May 1955, he was in the final for the very first time. In truth his first major singles final of any kind. The fact that he faced another Italian, Fausto Gardini, was no consolation – this was the big one and only a win for 'Beppe', as Merlo was known, would satisfy his dream.

Things started badly as Gardini stormed into the lead 6–1 but Merlo, determined not to let his chance slip by, took the second by the same emphatic score. When he took the third 6–3 to lead two sets to one he collected his thoughts for a final onslaught, just one set from victory.

The effort of it all was taking its toll and he began to suffer from the first signs of cramp as the fourth set progressed. But the prize was within his grasp and he moved ahead 6–5, just one game from victory.

Four points later the hurdle that had proved insurmountable in his career to date was down to just a single point as he advanced the score to 40–15. Two match points for the title.

Thirty-four games he'd played so far. Now just one little point would make Beppe the champion.

Maybe it was psychological, no one will ever know, but the leg cramps he'd been suffering suddenly took hold with a vengeance. He lost the first match point and let the second slip by. The leg cramps became more violent still as any attempts at stretching or pushing off quickly induced the agonizing and debilitating pain that only those who have suffered from cramps can imagine. From deuce he gamely continued but lost the next two points as well, as the score moved to 5–all in the fifth.

And there it finished. Merlo's dream had become a nightmare as the leg cramps took hold and he retired, quite unable to play on. He never did win the Italian Championship, or any major singles title.

Only the Frenchman Jean-Claude Molinari might claim an equally hard luck story. At the French Nationals in 1961 he looked to be about to satisfy French honour against American Fred Stolle as he led 6–4, 7–5, 5–2 and moved to 40–15 and two match points.

Only then did his Achilles tendon decide to rip and his retirement was inevitable. That, though, was a mere first-round match, and certainly not in the same league as Beppe's eleventh-hour demise.

Retirements or withdrawals midway through games and tournaments are naturally quite commonplace, but a couple more that certainly weren't are well worth recalling.

The American Beverley Fleitz, noted for her unusual ambidextrous style, had a definite chance at Wimbledon 1956. The year before, she'd taken the runners-up spot after losing so narrowly in the final to America's Louise Brough – 7–5, 8–6 was certainly tight and this time, seeded 2, she had a definite chance.

After a first-round bye she swept aside a Spaniard, a British player and a Hungarian without the loss of a set and was poised to face Britain's Angela Buxton in the quarter-finals. Feeling a little seedy before the match she sought out the tournament chairman Colin Gregory, a doctor by profession, for a consultation and immediately withdrew after his simple but surprise diagnosis – she was three months' pregnant.

Another terminal condition caused the enigmatic Danish player Torben Ulrich to retire mid-match in his third-round tie against America's Bill Hoepner in the Pacific Coast Tournament in Berkeley, California, in 1953. Ulrich was a graceful left-hander whose laid-back approach to both life and tennis was a legend on the circuit. To relax prior to a match at Wimbledon, getting away from the hustle and bustle, he once decided to practise his clarinet in a telephone box! Quite normal in Ulrich's world.

Hoepner was an irritating player much prone to meticulously tying up his laces and wiping his glasses at regular intervals. As if that wasn't annoying enough he was a habitual practitioner of the 'moonball', a mega-high and generally needless defensive lob.

Trailing 11–9 and 4–1 on one of Hoepner's most niggly days, Ulrich calmly walked to the net and shook hands: 'I quit,' he said. 'It wasn't any fun.'

It's the only known case of a player retiring from terminal boredom.

Ulrich's relaxed approach even extended to his own Danish Championship. In 1966 he again walked off court mid-match, this time to watch a World Cup football match on TV! Then again, he did win the title more times than he could remember.

If only poor Beppe Merlo could have hung loose just a fraction as much as Ulrich he might have added that elusive Italian title to his record. Instead he's remembered as the unluckiest loser in tennis history.

DISRUPTIVE DIANE

BOSTON, MASSACHUSETTS, AUGUST 1955

When members of the Longwood Cricket Club, founded near Boston in 1877, decided to lay a tennis court just a year later, they accepted on America's behalf surely their best ever import from Britain. The new lawn tennis centre thrived and America has never looked back.

But they ought to have realized that cricket grounds and the weather are notoriously bad mixers and that sooner or later the tennis would cop it too. Sure enough, in the summer of 1955, it was hit for six like never before or since.

When the seventy-fifth US National Doubles Championships began at Longwood on Monday 15 August no one anticipated anything out of the ordinary. High standards of tennis were expected, especially in the men's where all eyes would be on the leading American and Australian pairings who, five days after the tournament's scheduled finish on Sunday 21st, would meet in the Davis Cup final in New York.

The British entrants, who had decided to forego the delights of the Budleigh Salterton and New Malden tournaments back in England, didn't expect to progress far but at least they'd catch some decent weather and it would inevitably rain back home.

But no one had reckoned on a breezy lady named 'Diane' visiting Boston that August. The hurricane hit on the first Wednesday and for three whole days the rain lashed down. All the grass courts were flooded, some to above the net posts.

By Saturday, although matches had been switched indoors,

not even the first round was finished and the final should have been next day. But the tournament committee kept calm and announced that all matches from the quarter-finals onwards would be played on grass no matter how long it took.

The American Davis Cup players immediately withdrew and others with places to go quickly followed. Fourteen pairs scratched in all, plus another who conceded on their match point just to end the agony.

Soon only those with no prior commitments were left. That included the Brits and a keen but unseeded Japanese pair.

Disastrous as it was for the tennis, Hurricane Diane was a real tragedy for the nine states most severely hit. By Monday 22 August, 183 people were dead and 20,000 homeless. President Eisenhower declared a state of emergency, troops moved in and the Queen sent a message of sympathy.

Back in England the papers reported the disaster in a suitably grave manner, but the sports columns of *The Times* evidently saw the intervention of the tempestuous Diane as a boost for British tennis. Their Monday headline read: 'BECKER AND WILSON HAVE A CHANCE AS DAVIS CUP FINALISTS WITHDRAW IN U.S.' It's called clutching at straws.

Although play had started again outside by Tuesday, isolated showers were still proving troublesome and Roger Becker and Bobby Wilson had a lot of hanging around to do before their quarter-final on the road to expected British glory. Back in Blighty, meanwhile, the temperature reached 90 degrees in Budleigh Salterton and a mere 84 in New Malden.

Undeterred, the Brits in Boston accepted their soggy lot and disposed of two young Americans in a heroic 66-game quarter-final to advance to the semis, where only the unseeded Japanese blocked their way to the final.

If you're expecting the hollowest ever tournament victory in tennis history to go to the gallant Brits I'm afraid there's disappointment in store.

On Friday 26 August they were blown away by the unknown Atsushi Miyagi and Kosei Kamo in a stormy five-setter.

The Japanese duly went on to win the final and enter the record books as US doubles champions for 1955 after the most seriously disrupted event of all time.

NORMAL SERVICE WILL BE RESUMED AS SOON AS POSSIBLE

WIMBLEDON, JUNE 1957

It is the bane of the struggling club player's game, the *bête noire* of the habitual choker and an ever-present spectre for those of a nervous disposition. It is the double fault.

Everybody likes a second chance, whatever their field of endeavour. Back in 1877, when the triumvirate of lawn tennis lawmakers, Julian Marshall, Henry Jones and C. G. Heathcote, sat down to decide the precise code of rules for Wimbledon, their introduction of a 'permissible second service' was designed to help those who struggled to set the game in motion. Although all serves at that time were delivered either under-arm or round-arm rather than overhead, mistakes were common and it was felt that the one-serve rule prevailing before 1877 led to a rather disjointed game.

Yet incongruously, it was this 'helpful' rule concession that also created that very beast, the double fault, that has embarrassed tennis players ever since. Just ask the Brazilian player Miss Maria de Amorin.

They say the record books, like the camera, cannot lie. The record books show that on Tuesday 26 June 1957 Mrs L. B. E. Thung of Holland beat Miss M. H. de Amorin of Brazil 6–3, 4–6, 6–1 on Court 6 in the second round of the ladies' singles championships at Wimbledon.

Having received a bye in the first round it was the Brazilian's first match and the conclusion one must draw from

143

the result is that she performed creditably at the home of lawn tennis. She tailed off in the third, true, but she had certainly avoided the debutante's worst nightmare. She had not embarrassed herself. Or so the record books say. Now for the reality.

In her first service game Miss de Amorin started like many Wimbledon novices before and since, with a double fault. No disgrace in that, nor in the one that followed it immediately. But when two more gave her a round four the seeds of self-doubt must have begun to germinate.

Coaches tell us that the muscles tense, the elbow wobbles, the throw-up goes to pot, the head swims and the brain clouds when double faultitis takes hold. In her second service game Miss de Amorin was again left pointless, again from four more doubles. After 16 unsuccessful attempts to put a serve in, all the symptoms were surely taking hold.

The law of averages, if nothing else, would surely help her to find the service box in her third service game. But the Wimbledon dream was fast becoming a nightmare as another 8 attempts failed. She had served 12 double faults in a row.

Spectators are invariably a split camp in these situations. Some revel in the player's mounting discomfort while others feel so deeply for the sufferer they play every ball with them.

Both camps could take comfort, for while Miss de Amorin was missing with serves right, left, centre and into the net, her ground strokes during Mrs Thung's service games were not at all bad. On several occasions she broke back and as she began her fourth service game there was still hope.

She failed with the first two serves. Love–15. The umpire's voice must have echoed in her head. Two more failures followed. Love–30. She had been here before. Do they have Groundhog Day in Brazil? Seconds later it was Love–40.

Then game to Mrs Thung. Yet again, all of them doubles. It was now 16 in a row and Mrs Thung had yet to be called upon to hit a service return.

In her next service game Miss de Amorin maintained her remarkable consistency as two more serves failed to hit the mark; 17 double faults in a row.

144

Then, in this super-strange tennis match, the most amazing thing happened. Miss de Amorin got a serve in. The crowd reaction remains unrecorded. We'll settle for a balance of stunned silence, heavy sarcasm and gay abandon.

The set was lost 6–3. An ordinary score for an ordinary day. Do we still say the record books never lie?

Even more remarkably the Brazilian player, evidently massively uplifted by her new-found serving skills from the base line, recovered composure to take the second set 6–4. Only in the third set did she finally tail away.

She might take some comfort from knowing that it happens even to the best of them. The Croatian giant, Goran Ivanisevic, is one of the world's greatest ever servers. In 1996 he served more than 1,500 aces, yet in New Delhi in 1995 in his Davis Cup singles against India's Leander Paes he served 25 double faults, not far from a men's record. They weren't, though, all in a row.

The last words must go to Maria de Amorin. At her post-trauma interview, perhaps with a hint of understatement, she said without faltering: 'I was very nervous.'

BEGGING YOUR ROYAL PARDON

WIMBLEDON, JULY 1957

Something had been missing at Wimbledon since 1953. The patronage of the reigning monarch. Ever since the Prince of Wales and Princess Mary first visited the old Worple Road grounds in 1907, their royal visits had become a regular honour. As King George V and Queen Mary they attended in all but two years from 1919 to 1934 and after the king's death in 1936 Queen Mary missed just one meeting up to 1951.

Her son George VI, too, was an ardent fan. In 1926 he'd even competed, the only royal ever to do so, and he graced the 1947 Wimbledon with his knowledgeable presence in the company of his wife Queen Elizabeth, later the much revered Queen Mother.

When the king passed away in 1952 and his mother a year later, the Wimbledon authorities must have wondered if the new monarch, Queen Elizabeth II, would follow her father, mother and grandmother into the royal box.

Her husband, Prince Philip Duke of Edinburgh, had given it a go in 1953 and 1954 but the queen's interest seemed steadfastly nonexistent. At long last, in 1957, she was tempted to attend the ladies' singles and men's doubles finals on Saturday 6 July.

What followed was a hat trick of firsts, which was all very well as entertainment value up to a point, but the second of them was most definitely not in the Wimbledon script.

After seeing Althea Gibson become the first ever black

146

player to win a Wimbledon title Her Majesty settled into the men's doubles. It was a match *The Times* described as 'one from the top drawer' as the scratch American veteran pairing of Gardnar Mulloy and 'Budge' Patty became the first unseeded winners of a Wimbledon event. Their defeat of top-seeded Australians Lew Hoad and Neale Fraser 8–10, 6–4, 6–4, 6–4 was a true shock but their victory was only completed after a rude and unique interruption of the lunatic fringe variety.

The Life, Love and Sex Appeal Party was hardly going to challenge the Conservative government but its founder Helen Jarvis, of Northbrook Road, Croydon, evidently felt it had a voice. With Fraser and Hoad ahead at 5–4 in the first she used the change of ends to exercise the age-old right of a British subject to petition the monarch.

Hopping over the courtside wall, she raced to mid-court and faced Her Majesty head on, shouting and raving while holding up a bed sheet with a stitched message on it.

'WOMAN WAVES BANNER BEFORE THE QUEEN' reported *The Times*, which ambiguous headline begs the question as to what sort of banner Her Majesty was planning to wave later. 'Up the Aussies,' perhaps.

No one seemed entirely sure what Helen Jarvis wanted. Although she had the decency to preface her message with 'God Save Our Queen' she evidently wasn't a happy woman. Something along the lines of a complete revision of domestic politics and a revolutionary new world banking system seemed to be about the size of it.

The queen looked on stony-faced as the referee and a policeman hustled the unscheduled invader off court and arranged ongoing transport to Wimbledon police station, where Jarvis was held until the queen had left for Windsor Castle and then later released without charge.

Officially, little was said, but Wimbledon must have been embarrassed. It was fully five years before the queen entered the Wimbledon grounds again and thereafter another 15 before she attended the ladies' final in her Jubilee year of 1977 to see Britain's Virginia Wade claim a fairy-tale victory over the hapless Betty Stove.

147

A telling memory of that occasion comes from an unusual but reliable source, famous tennis habitué Sir Peter Ustinov, actor, writer and raconteur of world renown: 'I remember training my binoculars on the royal box at match point to our Ginny,' he wrote during Wimbledon 2000. 'The Queen was leafing through the pages of *Horse and Hound*. She has not been to Wimbledon since.'

So far as the queen's view of lawn tennis is concerned it must be assumed that the bizarre events of 1957 did nothing to create a convert. Evidently one is not amused.

A CHAMPAGNE MOMENT

ROLAND GARROS, PARIS, MAY 1958

The stylish 'Budge' Patty undoubtedly loved the French capital not just in the springtime but for the rest of the year too. This self-styled American in Paris chose to live there for many years.

But whether he liked it quite so much on Saturday 24 May 1958 must be a moot point.

It was the day he played French favourite Robert Haillet in the last 16 of the French Championships. Haillet never did win a major title whereas Patty had tasted victory in both the French and Wimbledon back in 1950 and, although 34, was still a force to be reckoned with.

French number two Haillet wasn't expected to win but he'd made the fatal mistake of playing out of his skin in the earlier rounds and the locals were aroused to a high pitch of expectation. That is more than can be said for the tennis correspondent of *The Times* whose seen-it-all-before style of reporting gave every impression of a hackneyed hack bored to tears.

Yet after this match he was moved to write that 'the whole thing was a masterpiece and I shall not expect to see anything more exciting for a very long time'.

The first four sets had been full of great tennis. Patty took the first 7–5 but Haillet, backed by a partisan Paris crowd, stormed back to take the next two 7–5 and 10–8. Seemingly tiring, though, he lost the fourth 6–4 and started the deciding fifth badly.

They had been on court three and a quarter hours when the point was reached at which even the most ardent Frenchman would have conceded the game was up. Haillet wasn't just down, he was surely out. He had slumped to 5–0 and now faced three match points at 40–0 on Patty's serve. He was as far behind as it's possible to be in a single set.

When he saved the first match point with a volley there was a ripple of applause. The backhand pass that saved the next elicited a little more enthusiasm and the forehand pass that took him to deuce caused the crowd to stir themselves afresh. Haillet took the game but still trailed 5–1.

Our friend from *The Times* later wrote: 'Miraculously he suddenly revived and there were so many moments worth recalling that one would need a volume for a full description.' We'll settle for a paragraph.

Haillet held serve, broke and held again to claw his way back to 5–4 but Patty, yet again serving for the match, looked to have stopped the rot as he moved to 40–15. But yet again Haillet used every shot in the book to hang on. A backhand pass, a smash, a drop shot and a forehand pass won him the game to level at 5–all.

Seven match points to the American had already gone begging.

Who better than *The Times* to talk us home?: 'Patty, assailed with cramp, disintegrated as Haillet swept home with two love games to such a roar as the Roland Garros Stadium had not heard all week. After this the remaining matches were as water to champagne.'

The score in the record books reads 5–7, 7–5, 10–8, 4–6, 7–5. What a story it hides. No matter that Haillet lost in straight sets in the quarter-final three days later. He had come back from the brink in front of his own crowd in the greatest revival of all time.

THE ROMAN CIRCUS

FORO ITALICO, ROME, MAY 1963

It was David Gray, writing for the *Guardian*, who described the match he'd just seen as 'a Roman circus'. And he'd seen a few matches in his time. But then this one has gone down in lawn-tennis history not for the quality of the play but for the lack of quality of its officials.

Britain's Davis Cup player Tony Pickard knew that his second-round Italian Championships clash against New Zealand's Ian Crookenden wouldn't be easy, but by the time the papers were printing the headline 'PICKARD LOSES AMID PANDEMONIUM' he knew that playing tennis in Rome presented difficulties of a very peculiar kind.

Don't we all love the Italians, though. Their enthusiasm for life, their *al fresco* lunches, the constant babble of conversation – it's that lively approach that makes them all so charming and lovable.

Tennis court protocol, of course, requires a certain sort of disciplined behaviour. The crowd must be fair and reasonably quiet, umpires must keep control and linesmen must be forever watchful. Except when the game's in Rome!

It was a typically hot and dusty scene on Tuesday 7 May as the players took to the red clay of the famous Foro Italico. Right from the start there were some dodgy line calls and the crowd, eating, drinking and talking animatedly, gave every impression of being at a picnic. The tennis was purely a sideline.

The linesmen didn't want to be left out. Several times both Pickard and Crookenden complained to the umpire about linesmen indulging in long conversations with stray spectators during play. At one stage Crookenden started calling his own lines and the *Daily Telegraph* correspondent insists to this day that Pickard lost at least one vital point because a linesman failed to call 'out' a ball which landed 9 inches beyond a line – he was leaning over the fence buying an ice-cream at the time.

Nor were the ballboys any more disciplined. They constantly scurried around court during rallies. Then again, so did the linesmen.

The Coca-Cola man, too, seemed to have been granted the freedom of the court as he interrupted play several times to restock the refrigerator by the umpire's chair.

But it was thirsty work out there; witness the *Guardian* match report:

> The most astonishing moment amidst umpiring of an alarming inefficiency came towards the end of the fourth set. In the middle of a game just as Pickard was about to serve, the scoreboard operator called for a drink. A linesman immediately crossed the court and spent some time trying to get the bottle to him, as he was just out of reach on a stand. Pickard put down his racket and watched incredulously.

When asked about the incident later the umpire was reported to have said: 'You must remember, it was very hot out there.'

As for the progress of the match, Pickard took the first set 6–4 and was twice within two points of a two set lead before losing the second set 7–5. He regained the lead by taking the third 9–7 but, with concentration and spirits flagging, he lost the last two sets 6–1, 6–2.

Several respected tennis correspondents have described the overall officiating at the match as the worst they have ever witnessed.

Nor was it just a one off. Two days later the Australian

number two Ken Fletcher got so fed up with a spectator who would insist on talking to his Brazilian opponent Fernandes during play that he finally retorted: 'One more time and I'll punch you on the nose.'

The umpire looked on unconcerned.

The British player Bobby Wilson, meanwhile, didn't even have an umpire when his game was scheduled to start. For half an hour in the scorching afternoon sun he knocked up with Mulligan, his Australian opponent, before walking off in disgust. Mulligan carried on hitting with a ballboy. When the umpire did turn up he explained he had been having a nap and had 'overslept'.

During the match he asked the crowd for quiet only for an indignant spectator to answer him back: 'We have paid for our seats so we have a right to say a few words!'

On top of it all, many games were played entirely without ballboys and in the last 16 of the ladies' doubles, 6 games at the start of one of the matches were umpired by a player when, surprise, surprise, the requisite official was conspicuous by his absence.

All this, remember, in one of the most highly ranked tournaments outside the four Grand Slam events. And for every incident that has been documented, there are sure to be many that haven't.

Not to put too fine a point on it, the whole thing was a shambles.

Next time you wonder if the officials at Wimbledon might just be a little too disciplined, think of Rome 1963 and be thankful for small mercies.

DOROTHY'S NIGHTMARE

WIMBLEDON, JUNE 1964

It's every tennis-lover's dream to be immortalized at Wimbledon. Dorothy Cavis-Brown loved tennis but the fame she achieved on 22 June 1964, opening day, was for her nothing but a recurring nightmare.

Mrs Cavis-Brown hadn't travelled far from her Chelsea home to act as lineswoman for the first-round match on Court 3. All the better to arrive fresh and mentally attuned for the big-hitting affair between South Africa's Abie Segal and Clark Graebner of the United States.

Linespersons have been accused of many spurious misdemeanours over the years but the fate that befell Cavis-Brown is graphically true and photographs of the incriminating moment are still being published today.

Segal was coasting at 6–2, 7–5, 5–2, serving at match point. He served, met the return with a firm volley and saw Graebner's attempted pass go wide into the tramlines by around a foot. Segal advanced to the net to shake hands but Graebner stood his ground.

Segal's definitive account goes like this:

'Graebner stands there and says: "Where are you going, Abie? Nobody's called 'out'. The rules say that if nobody calls 'out' the game isn't over."'

'Suddenly I realize he's right, so I turn round to see what's going on.'

The sight that met Segal's eyes was a memorable one.

154

Dorothy Cavis-Brown was fast asleep, arms folded, one leg crossed, head lolled, and all at an angle which made the leaning tower of Pisa look stable.

By now there was much nudging and tittering in the crowd as the umpire asked a sheepish ballboy to go up and prod her. Meanwhile Segal and Graebner were still musing at the net. Tongue firmly in cheek Graebner persisted: 'She's still supposed to call "out".'

'So I go up to the linesman to help the ballboy,' recalled Segal: '"Hey, madam!" I say, "do you mind callin' 'out'," and suddenly her eyes open: "Out," she calls, and points with her arm.'

Segal's statement to the press was to the point: 'I always knew my game was boring, but I didn't think it was that bad! In Italy they fall asleep all the time, but never on match point.'

The tabloids had fun at Mrs Cavis-Brown's expense but she got off lightly by today's standards. Her own statement was not altogether convincing: 'I think I became a little dizzy, a little drowsy. I am overtired. I have had a very exhausting time just lately. Doing a lot of work.'

Tournament referee Captain Michael Gibson backed her up officially: 'We understand about all this and she has the committee's confidence. She is very experienced.'

Behind closed doors, though, there was hushed talk of a liquid lunch. Gin was mentioned. Whatever the truth, Dorothy Cavis-Brown never sat the lines at Wimbledon again.

Segal, though, one of the game's great talkers, was happy to relate the yarn to anyone on his world travels who would listen. Thus Wimbledon immortality was doubly assured for Dorothy Cavis-Brown.

A GAME OF TWO HALVES

EXMOUTH, AUGUST 1966

It was a brave tournament referee indeed who agreed to take on the National Under-14 and Under-16 Lawn Tennis Championships in the summer of 1966.

Run in tandem with the Exmouth Junior Championships, that meant coping with 250 competitors, and their doting parents, and scheduling more than 700 matches. One of them, Diane Bridger, would play the most unusual match of her career.

The weather would be crucial. As generations of Devon holidaymakers know only too well, the glorious sunshine of the brochures isn't always guaranteed. The sun may have shone on England's World Cup winning football team just a few days before but for the summer game the weather did what comes naturally. At the seaside resort of Exmouth the referee's spades of optimism were quickly dampened as incessant rain came down in buckets.

Opening day had been at least tolerable but on the Tuesday of the championships only three matches were completed as play was abandoned for the day shortly after lunch with a total of only 170 matches finished so far.

Even when it stopped, the Exmouth grass courts were just too sodden. The *Guardian* reported the referee's stiff-upper-lip response. 'It is a disappointing position but by no means hopeless,' he said, struggling manfully to remain upbeat.

Frantic calls were made to nearby Exeter Golf Club, who

156

eased the position by making their hard courts available for the next day's play. Although only 12 miles away further up the estuary, the localized weather, too, had been much better there. In fact there were even reports of sunshine.

It was on Wednesday 3 August that one of Devon's local favourites, Diane Bridger, decamped from Exmouth to Exeter to take on Lancashire girl Marilyn Bevan in the third round of the Under-16 girls' singles.

Starting in the morning she began well on the golf club's hard courts and stormed through the first set 6–1. In fact 'stormed' was the operative word, because again the rains came with a vengeance.

But the British weather is nothing if not fickle. Back at Exmouth 'the sun had mercifully broken through' and the grass courts were dry enough for play.

With playing time at a premium there was only one thing for it; the girls piled into a car and made the 12-mile dash for Exmouth, arriving in time for an afternoon slot.

There, cool as the proverbial cucumber, Diane finished the job by taking the second set 6–2.

It was, as they say, a 'game of two halves'. The Devon girl had proved herself on two surfaces in the same match played 12 miles apart in the morning and afternoon of the same day.

The next day's newspaper headline was even more predictable than a Devon downpour: 'MISS BRIDGER TRAVELS FAR FOR VICTORY.'

MATCH OF THE DAY

WIMBLEDON, JULY 1967

Saturday 1 July 1967 was an important day for Britain's Roger Taylor. The ruggedly handsome son of a Yorkshire miner had reached the last 16 at Wimbledon. Only three British men since the war, Tony Mottram, Mike Sangster and Bobby Wilson, had gone further and the Wimbledon faithful needed a new hero.

Standing in Taylor's way for a place in the last 8 that day was the South African Cliff Drysdale, seeded number 5.

Journalists were fond of describing Drysdale as 'debonair' and there was no doubt that he had the sort of matinée-idol looks that attracted more than his fair share of female admirers.

As Saturday dawned there was no real reason why such a young, free and single spirit should be feeling trepidation but those who knew Drysdale might just have detected a hint of nerves as he prepared for his match.

Any doubts he was feeling might equally have seemed unnecessary to anyone who had studied the form book, for wasn't it Drysdale who in the Davis Cup at Eastbourne just two years previously had swept Taylor aside 6–1, 6–2, 7–5? The British player had been described by one disgruntled pressman on that occasion as 'clumsy and inept'.

Maybe it was the sense of occasion that was getting to Drysdale. He was, after all, preparing to enter an arena of some sanctity. All eyes would be on him. Might he panic in the face of such scrutiny? Might the gathered throng give him the thumbs down? The Centre Court could, after all, be an intimidating place.

Drysdale began well, taking the first set 6–3, but Taylor fought back doggedly to win the second 11–9 and the third 6–4. Those watching detected Drysdale's unease and a certain distraction but he dug in to level the match, winning the fourth set 6–4. By the end of the fifth the pressmen were already writing their 'Match of the Day' headlines, penning the copy that the next day's readers would devour as 'the gritty Yorkshireman gained his revenge, bludgeoning the South African, denying him rhythm as he lost much of his poise'.

They were right. Taylor took the final set 6–4 for a famous British victory.

The *Guardian* particularly noted that this had been a different Drysdale from the one they knew: 'No one recognized the South African on Saturday afternoon as the suave competitor who destroyed Tony Roche last year,' said their reporter David Gray.

He was nearer the mark than most of their readers knew for Drysdale was indeed a different man even from the one who'd looked in the mirror that very morning.

Unbeknown to many, on his way to the Centre Court, he'd already successfully negotiated another vital match, a doubles which was arguably the most important of his life.

The Drysdale that stepped on to Centre Court in the afternoon was, in fact, an entirely different species. A married man!

The real match of the day had taken place that morning at Paddington Registry Office when fellow South African Jean Forbes, sister of Cliff's Davis Cup colleague Gordon Forbes, had been more than delighted to consent to have her name changed to Mrs Jean Drysdale.

It was the strangest preparation for a tennis match in the annals of the game and it surely makes Britain's heroic Roger Taylor the biggest wedding-day gooseberry of all time.

TENNIS RE-INVENTED

KANSAS CITY, OKLAHOMA, FEBRUARY 1968

Back in the psychedelic 1960s, rejecting traditional values was just one big trip. And what better target than stuffy old tennis?

New Orleans entrepreneur Dave Dixon didn't know too much about the game but he had a track record of knowing what the public wanted and giving it to them big time. He'd done it in plywood and American football and figured tennis was just another product that needed re-inventing. It's thanks to Dixon that tennis experienced one of its strangest nights ever one freezing February in Kansas City, 1968.

The game, he argued, was dull, colourless and boring and the crowds were far too sedate. There were some great players out there but they were playing on the wrong stage: 'How can a sport become a mass spectator game if all the best moves have to be watched in silence?' he preached.

He declared his intention to give the game colour, alter its antiquated scoring system and take it into comfortable weatherproof indoor arenas where packed crowds would hoot and holler to their hearts' content. He gave the game World Championship Tennis.

The eight players that formed the Dixon circus on the opening night of a planned grand tour of 80 venues had been hand-picked. Talented tennis players and all good-lookers. Aiming to capture the women's market, Dixon dubbed them 'The Handsome Eight'.

They'd get the show on the road with a World Cup competition at the American Royal Arena on Friday 2 February.

Roger Taylor, Nikki Pilic, John Newcombe, Tony Roche, Cliff Drysdale, Dennis Ralston, Pierre Barthes and Butch Buccholz didn't take much persuading; around 100,000 dollars was their projected take for the whole tour. They'd do anything for that sort of money, which was just as well.

The scoring was ping-pong style, 31 up per set. If sets were tied at one-all it was straight into a best of nine points sudden death. As for the kit, it was positively 'no whites'. Players would win instant cash depending on results and hushed crowds would simply not be tolerated: 'At no point will our umpires demand silence,' roared Dixon; 'Not an evening for the traditionalists,' headlined the *Guardian*, adding with just a hint of trepidation that 'apart from the tennis itself, WCT rejects almost everything else that is part of the normal game.'

Just in case the crowds fell below the required decibel rate, incentives were offered. Sponsors Revlon got in 3,000 bottles of perfume and after-shave to give away to those who shouted their man to victory. Revlon knew it was working when they ran a pilot a week earlier in Australia; as the women's choice Roger Taylor, 'the Red Baron' on account of his scarlet kit, broke serve against Barthes, an Aussie in the crowd evidently desperate for his after-shave jumped up, yelling, 'Drop dead Pommie!' Wimbledon it certainly wasn't.

Just as bizarre as the game was the venue. The Royal Arena was far from regal. It was an ice-rink adjacent to the slaughter house in the Kansas stockyards and the astro-turf court was laid straight over the ice. British tennis correspondent David Gray was not impressed: 'Outside it was two degrees below zero and inside even colder,' he told *Guardian* readers, adding graphically for good measure that 'Kansas City makes Wolverhampton look like Athens.'

As for the matches themselves, the opening honour, appropriately enough, went to America's own Dennis Ralston who defeated Frenchman Barthes, representing Europe, by the then unique score of 31–27, 31–29.

And that was just the start. Later in the night Ralston ran for a lob and overshot the carpet, sliding on the ice before crashing into a linesman's chair. The crowd loved it. Maybe the players were unsure; one press report stated without a hint of irony that 'John Newcombe wore brown trousers for his opening game.'

Between matches a dance group performed 'The Serve', described by one bemused journalist as 'a rock and roll routine comprising boys and girls hitting ambidextrous forehands and spasmodic volleys'.

Did the crowd go home happy? Apparently so, but there were only 1,000 there. Dixon's vision certainly didn't come into the glorious focus he'd imagined but World Championship Tennis succeeded in its own peculiar way in breaking the vicarage-garden-party mould of tennis for ever.

Although there was to be much modification and Dixon soon sold his stake after a few almighty flops (including an occasion in Shreveport, Louisiana, when the players and crowd turned up but someone forgot to bring the court), the strange night of 2 February 1968 changed the permissible boundaries of tennis and heralded the Open era we enjoy today.

LOSER TAKES ALL

FOREST HILLS, NEW YORK, SEPTEMBER 1968

A long-running tennis controversy was resolved in 1968 when the era of Open tennis was officially sanctioned, allowing professionals into the major tournaments to compete alongside the amateurs for prize money set to reach new heights.

On the face of it everyone was a winner. The top class pros frozen out of the majors for years could now show what they could do against the best amateurs. The amateurs, meanwhile, who had long belied their nominal status by accepting 'expenses' for all and sundry, could at last come out of the closet and legitimately accept real prize money while having a pop at the pros into the bargain.

A world with no losers, surely. But there's nothing so strange as tennis politics for turning the game on its head. Take the case of Arthur Ashe and the first US Open in 1968.

Although the Open era had kicked off in the rather unglamorous confines of the British Hard Court Championships at Bournemouth in April, results there had set everybody talking and by the time the French Open and Wimbledon had passed successfully, with some superb matches and dramatic shocks en route, all eyes turned to the States for what would be the biggest pot of the season.

The sum of 14,000 dollars for the winner of the men's singles might not sound much now but it was certainly money the United States Amateur Champion Arthur Ashe could have used to supplement his income as an army lieutenant. Back in

1968 it was the biggest cash prize in the world but the field was strong and his chances of seeing off the big guns seemed very slim.

The fates, though, looked like being kind to the talented black American as 14 of the leading professionals were toppled in the first week. Meanwhile Ashe played sublime tennis and went all the way to the final where the 'Flying Dutchman' Tom Okker stood between him and a slice of history – not to mention the cash.

Ashe did make history on the fabled lawns of Forest Hills on that Monday 9 September. In a classic match and a marvellous display of tennis he beat Ocker 14–12, 5–7, 6–3, 3–6, 6–3 to become the first winner of the US Open and the first ever black man to win the United States title.

No one doubted he deserved his reward. Unfortunately, thanks to the politicians, he didn't get it!

Keen to play Davis Cup for America, Ashe had made sure to preserve his amateur status as a necessary qualification at that time. His reward for such patriotism was an eleventh-hour decision by the United States Lawn Tennis Association, still rather befuddled by the whole amateur-professional debate, that their amateurs couldn't yet accept prize money!

The loser Tom Okker was duly presented with a fat winner's cheque for 14,000 dollars. The *Guardian* described this in rather guarded terms as 'a curious situation' while tennis journalist Richard Evans in his book *Open Tennis* said simply: 'The sporting world acclaimed a new hero but also laughed at the absurdity of a sport that gave the loser the prize money and the winner nothing.'

The comments of many others are not deemed fit for family consumption. Suffice it to say, once in a while it's the ludicrous doings of tennis politicians that give the players automatic entry into the world of strange matches.

THE GONZALES MATCH

WIMBLEDON, JUNE 1969

There's never been a more memorable decade for stop-in-your-tracks headlines than the 1960s. KENNEDY ASSASSINATED and THE GREAT TRAIN ROBBERY stunned TV viewers and newspaper readers in 1963, CHURCHILL DEAD marked the end of an era in 1965 and just a year later ABERFAN DISASTER worked its shocking and lasting effect. On a happier note, ENGLAND'S WORLD CUP from 1966 and MAN ON THE MOON from 1969 were both astonishing in different ways (strange to think that the first of those headlines would now be more startling than the second!) but what is most remarkable about these collective recollections from the Swinging Sixties is that they are so often joined in people's memories by a mere first-round tennis match at Wimbledon.

Only an extraordinary and romantic contest could keep the company of such pivotal events and be so clearly recalled more than 30 years on by so many who witnessed it – Ricardo Alonzo 'Pancho' Gonzales v. Charlie Pasarell was exactly that.

It was, on paper, nothing more than a routine opening match between a great old master and the former pupil 16 years his junior. Gonzales, Los Angeles born but of Mexican origin, had been US singles champion way back in 1948 and 1949 before turning professional and establishing himself as what many regarded as the world's best player throughout the 1950s.

Wimbledon's closure to professionals had kept him out of the world's greatest tournament until it went Open in 1968 and then he crashed in the third round to the Soviet player Alexander Metrevelli. Surely he was a spent force. In 1969 he'd be 41.

Puerto-Rican-born Charlie Pasarell, in contrast, was a muscular 25-year-old making waves in the game and still with a future ahead of him. In his junior days, Gonzales had coached him.

Play began on Centre Court at around half past six on Tuesday 24 June. After a first Monday completely washed out, the committee must have been hopeful they could get the match finished before close of play.

Gonzales had other ideas – from 5–4 down in the first he served to keep the set alive 18 times, saving 11 set points along the way before losing it in very gloomy light by a remarkable 24–22.

Dripping with sweat, his body and face gaunt in the half-light, Gonzales expected play to finish for the day, as did the crowd. He was visibly astonished when tournament referee Mike Gibson commanded play to continue and started the second set in the blackest of moods as nine o'clock loomed.

'He prowled the baseline like some caged and tormented lion,' wrote one reporter.

When it began to drizzle his glower deepened and he appealed loudly to the umpire: 'How can I play when I can't see?' he demanded. The umpire remained unmoved and amidst continued ranting, raving and racket throwing (more shocking in those pre-McEnroe days) Gonzales did nothing more than go through the motions and was blown away 6–1 in less than 15 minutes. Only then was a halt called as he 'stormed off scowling, his face tinted a sort of green in the light giving him the air of some great Aztec god, an awesome, fearsome sight'. TV viewers would never forget it.

Tuesday's play had certainly been thrilling and dramatic but, when they started again at two o'clock on Wednesday, everybody's expectation was that Pasarell would finish him off quickly. But again it was nip and tuck and Gonzales took the set 16–14, Pasarell finishing with two double faults, his first real sign of weakness.

Gonzales, still fit and resilient despite his age, fortified by a night's sleep and buoyed by the crowd's cheers, smelt blood. He took the next set 6–3, Pasarell again finishing with a double fault.

At 2 sets all it now seemed a matter of endurance and Gonzales, by now with dew drops of sweat dripping from his angular nose, hanging his head, leaning on his racket, looked spent. The quality of play remained astonishingly high but eventually Pasarell led 5–4 and forced his one-time mentor to 0–40 on his own serve.

But two Pasarell lobs landed inches out and Gonzales saved the third match point with an ace. Seven deuces later he was back to 5–all but then quickly falling behind 5–6, again serving to save the match and slipping once more to 0–40.

Just one point for Pasarell would do it but a smash, an angled volley and a serve astonishingly got Gonzales off the hook yet again as the crowd and TV viewers alike became near-hysterical.

The reserves of energy of the veteran were remarkable but surely not inexhaustible and, facing his seventh match point at 7–8, Gonzales moved to the net on obviously tired legs. As another Pasarell lob left him for dead it all looked over but once more the ball landed a fraction long.

That was the point at which the younger man's spirit seemed to leave him, as the iron will and forceful personality of Gonzales won him 11 consecutive points. After 5 hours and 20 minutes' play over two days, embracing a Wimbledon record of 112 games, Gonzales clinched the set 11–9 on his first match point.

He had won 22–24, 1–6, 16–14, 6–3, 11–9. No matter that he eventually went out to Arthur Ashe in the last 16. 'Pancho' Gonzales had shown Wimbledon what they'd been missing. For its combination of sheer drama, courage, passion, skill and emotion 'the Gonzales match', as even casual tennis fans simply call it, is still regarded by many as the greatest of all time.

A STING IN THE TAIL

FOREST HILLS, NEW YORK, SEPTEMBER 1969

To the uninitiated, the West Side Tennis Club, Forest Hills, Queens, New York, might sound like a tranquil address for a quiet game of tennis. Back in the 1920s it surely was but by the Open era it was a different story.

'The distractions were extraordinary,' wrote a startled English journalist in 1969: 'There was the umpire's booming voice, the cries of refreshment salesmen, the roar of aircraft, the chugging of helicopters and the clatter of the Long Island railroad.'

Not a place for the over-sensitive for sure, but someone like the affable Australian Karen Krantzcke wasn't phased by such things. Weighing in at over 12 stone, 6 feet 2 inches tall, with a rather ploddy splay-footed gait, and brutally dismissive strokes, she was a tough cookie but set about everything with such a genial serenity that her popularity was assured. It took more than a bit of Big Apple mayhem to put 'Kran' off her game.

Or less, perhaps, for sometimes even the biggest personalities can be completely knocked off their stride by the smallest of things.

That was exactly the case on Tuesday 2 September as Krantzcke and her Australian partner Kerry Melville faced fellow Aussies Gail Chanfreau and Leslie Hunt in a second-round match at the 1969 US Open.

Chanfreau and Hunt took the first set 6–4 but Krantzcke and

Melville, amidst all the noises off, ground out the second 7–5. As they prepared for the decider Krantzcke took a swig of her Sportade energy drink and heard a buzz which alarmed her. It seemed a bee, too, fancied a drink.

Before she could take evasive action Kran was stung on the lip by the pesky creature and prepared for what she knew would be the outcome, for she was allergic to bee stings. Out came the rash as she began to feel unwell, and she retired before hitting another ball.

It is the only time a bee has knocked someone out of the US Open, but a swarm of the little devils invaded Centre Court at Wimbledon with an impressive display of formation flying on Wednesday 2 July 1958, again during a doubles. This time a men's between Indian pairing R. Krishnan and N. Kumar and the title holders Budge Patty and Gardnar Mulloy of the US.

The Indians lost the first 6–3, took the next two 6–4, 6–2, lost the fourth 6–3 and moved to 6–5 in the decider. It was just as Patty prepared to serve to save the match that the bee squadron moved in, causing only a short delay but perhaps enough to disturb the American's concentration. A few points later, with Mulloy hitting two straightforward smashes out, it was game, set and match to the Indians – or was it the bees?

Now we're on the wildlife trail, there has to be a mention, too, of the 1949 second-round singles at Wimbledon in which the Dutchman Hans van Swol faced France's Robert Abdesselam. With the match tied at 2 sets all, the Frenchman moved to 5–3 in the decider and van Swol looked beaten. That was the point a squirrel chose to make his entrance, leading the ballboys a merry dance for fully three minutes before they saw it off.

Having reclined on the grass for the duration, van Swol came back to 5–5 and eventually took the set 13–11: 'That squirrel sure helped me,' he said afterwards, and as a tribute to the valiant animal he had one embroidered on his shirt at the next year's tournament.

The real sting in the tail, though, takes us back to Karen Krantzcke, this time to Tallahassee, Florida, on Sunday 10 April 1977, where she had just clinched another ladies' doubles title to add to her haul.

If you're expecting alligators, forget it. This was much worse. Shortly after the match, Kran announced she was going for a quick warm-down jog, but collapsed 200 yards from the court. Two doctors who had watched her match failed to revive her.

A heart attack, the deadliest foe of all, had beaten Karen Krantzcke without even a warning. She was only 30.

ROCKET'S DAMP SQUIB

FOREST HILLS, NEW YORK, SEPTEMBER 1969

They called him 'Rocket Rod' for good reasons. Not only because he came from Rockhampton in North Queensland but also for the pace, style and fizz with which he played the game. Those who saw him as a boy in the late 1940s said the sky was the limit for the bandy-legged left-hander and they were right. Rod Laver grew up to make tennis history.

Achieving the Grand Slam as an amateur in 1962 was a milestone. Only one man before him, the American Donald Budge, had held the Wimbledon, US, Australian and French titles at the same time, way back in 1938.

Many great players had tried and failed since, so Laver's achievement was no mean feat. When he turned professional in 1963 he was barred from the Grand Slam events but when the major championships became Open in 1968 he simply took up where he left off.

As he approached the 1969 US Open at Forest Hills he'd already bagged three majors that year and a win on the New York grass would give him a place in history as the only man to win the Grand Slam twice.

Such a historic tennis moment surely deserved a dazzling sun, perfectly manicured greensward and capacity crowd, but history is a fickle customer. The 'Rockhampton Rocket' did pull it off, but only in the midst of some of the strangest scenes ever witnessed at a Grand Slam final.

Contrary to popular folklore it's not just Wimbledon that

171

suffers rain and the English referee Captain Mike Gibson must have been cursing his luck as the famous Forest Hills courts were regularly soaked. And when play was possible they began to churn up so badly that one English reporter was moved to describe conditions as 'ludicrous, with the turf spongy, balls heavy and divots flying all over the place'.

Innovation was the order of the day as Margaret Court and Virginia Wade completed their semi-final match wearing socks over their pumps to gain a grip on what was left of the slithery turf. Even New York's old cosmetic trick of spraying the courts green couldn't have helped this year. There was almost more mud than grass.

Play lingered on into a third damp week and it wasn't until Monday 8 September that Rodney George Laver got his chance to make history against fellow Australian Tony Roche. As a vastly depleted crowd waited for a rain-delayed start, referee Captain Gibson, keen to get the 'Rocket' on court, played a master stroke of his own.

No one present would ever forget the bizarre sight of a helicopter hovering perilously above the Stadium Court to create a drying wind: 'HELICOPTER SPIN-DRIES COURT' read an unlikely headline in the next day's paper.

And they would always remember Laver changing into spikes as he let the first set slither away from him on a churned-up court which *The Times* described as 'like a farmyard after the cows have come home'.

When Laver himself finally came home via a historic 7–9, 6–1, 6–2, 6–2 victory he attributed the win, with typical modesty, to his timely change of footwear. But good tennis judges knew better.

A damp squib of an occasion it may have been but they'd seen a master at work and were privileged to have been present for this rather surreal piece of lawn tennis history.

A TASTE OF INDIA

MADRAS GYMKHANA CLUB, APRIL 1973

When the Australians were drawn to play India away in the Davis Cup Eastern Zone final of 1973, none of them expected an easy ride.

Skulduggerous practice was par for the course everywhere in that competition and India, moreover, was always regarded as a bit risky, even by Aussies with lager-hardened stomachs and an in-built confidence to ply their trade any time, anywhere and against anyone. But what they actually got exceeded their worst nightmares.

They didn't really expect beautifully manicured grass and, even though the Indians were quite capable of delivering it, the hosts didn't like to disappoint their guests. Lawn tennis, after all, had long since been played on many different surfaces – clay, sand, gravel, concrete, shale, ash, tarmac, rubber, wood, tiles, carpet, parquet blocks – it was just a case of what ingredients they'd opt for.

Their recipe was imaginative enough. Starting with a foundation of sand and brick, then overlaying fine gravel, they topped it off with a layer of surface clay appetizingly mixed with liberal helpings of ripe cow dung, all left to bake hard under the fierce midday sun.

At least they had no trouble finding the courts: 'Just follow yer nose mate' was the Aussie cry.

Equally keen to live up to their reputation in the matter of stadium design, the Indians had lost no time in commissioning the construction of a state-of-the-art arena at the Madras

173

Gymkhana Club – unfortunately, the state-of-the-art 1973 style was distinctly Primitive School. The whole 15,000-capacity stadium was built in just ten days; timber poles and planks were lashed together, using the odd nail here and there where real strength was needed and the whole thing was topped off with a roof of dried palm fronds. Health and safety inspectors and fire officers were not part of the package.

Yet, strange as this venue was for what was, after all, the twentieth and not the nineteenth century, that wasn't the worst of it for the gallant Australians.

As the veteran squad (they called them Dad's Army) – of Newcombe, Anderson, Masters, Giltinan and Cooper – arrived in Madras, they were not so much given a warm welcome as a pretty darn hot one. The Pakistani terrorist group Black December had issued death threats against them as part of an effort to get the Indian government to release 90,000 Pakistani prisoners of war. By way of a warm up they'd blown up an airline office a few days before.

If ever the resolve of a tennis team had been tested this was surely it, but the Australians agreed to stay after a personal guarantee of safety was offered by the assistant commissioner of police. The upshot of that was that all the players were confined to their hotel except for visits to court and all forays to the stadium were accompanied by a van full of armed police. Meals were checked for poison, police with machine guns guarded the visitors day and night and all letters and packages were intercepted. Always at the players' side was the best sharp-shooter the Madras police could muster – dressed in casual civvies, his ever-present sunhat certainly looked the part but actually concealed his revolver.

It is to the eternal credit of the Australians that they overcame what must surely rank as the worst conditions ever to prevail at a Davis Cup match to win the tie without losing a rubber. They went on to win the trophy that year, taking the Indian Experience in their stride like true pros.

The story that John Newcombe, asked to sum up the trip in a few words, simply replied that 'The courts were crap', is almost certainly apocryphal.

174

BATTLE OF THE SEXES

HOUSTON, TEXAS, SEPTEMBER 1973

The game between Bobby Riggs and Billie Jean King was the Battle of the Sexes par excellence. Hype, needle, glamour, a live worldwide TV audience of millions, and yet more hype . . . it was the game that promised everything.

They called Robert Larimore Riggs 'the Hustler' for good reason. He would bet on anything, but particularly himself. Arriving at Wimbledon for the first time in 1939 he strolled anonymously into a London bookmaker's and backed 'Riggs to win all three titles'. Two weeks later he strolled out again with the singles, doubles and mixed in the bag, leaving a stunned bookmaker counting his losses.

At Wembley arena shortly after the war he vowed to beat the Irish Davis Cup player Lyttleton Rogers without ever venturing beyond the service box line. 'And it will be a whitewash,' he added. The game was duly won 6–0, 6–0.

Nor did Riggs mellow with age. By 55, he had cultivated a new image as the game's leading Male Chauvinist Pig and, to prove superiority, he challenged 30-year-old Australian Margaret Court to a one-off singles. Court was a powerful and gritty athlete who took the US, Australian and French titles in 1973 and would retire in 1977 with 67 Grand Slam titles under her belt. Her only weakness was an occasional susceptibility to nerves. Riggs worked on that and, on 13 May 1973, in Ramona near San Diego, California, he chipped, lobbed and floated his way to easy victory, 6–2, 6–1.

175

He presented Margaret with flowers. She curtsied. Feminists groaned. They called it 'the Mother's Day Massacre' but as a spectacle it was an almighty flop. Probably the strangest thing about that match was the name of one of the official photographers, Ivor Bollockoff.

Riggs crowed to anyone who would listen, declaring himself 'the hero of middle-aged men, leader of Bobby's Battalions and world undisputed No. 1 male chauvinist.' Fellow pigs loved it.

But followers of the ever-strengthening Women's Movement hated it, and none more so than 29-year-old Billie Jean King whose list of titles is legendary. After initially refusing Riggs's challenge she agreed to the Battle of the Sexes determined to teach her fellow Californian a lesson.

The match would be a five-set 100,000-dollar contest. Riggs milked the pre-game publicity for all it was worth: 'I'm so confident of winning that if I lose I'll jump off the Pasadena suicide bridge,' he boasted. Just to make sure, he was popping 415 vitamin pills a day.

The game had never seen anything like it. A record tennis crowd of 30,492 turned out at Houston Astrodome baseball stadium on the evening of 20 September 1973. To those in the six-dollar seats at the back, the court was a mere pinprick. Those in the 100-dollar courtside seats shared a close-up view with a worldwide TV audience of nearly 50 million.

The spectacle began with a grand entrance straight from an MGM blockbuster. A group of servile footballers carried King on to court on a triumphal litter decorated with gold cherubs and pink ostrich feathers. She duly presented Riggs with a live piglet.

Not to be outdone, Riggs was borne into the arena on a rickshaw pulled by six scantily clad nubiles dubbed 'Bobby's Bosom Buddies'. He was dressed as Henry VIII and gnawed on a huge bone while presenting King with a giant dummy and the oily line 'You're going to be a sucker for my lobs.'

It was the day circus, carnival and theatre met lawn tennis head on. It was a day, too, that Riggs might have regretted. His puff-ball tactics didn't fool Billie Jean. She attacked relentlessly and Riggs was forced to run. Looking every year of his 55, and something like a cross between Woody Allen and Sergeant Bilko, he was humbled in straight sets 6–4, 6–3, 6–3.

The Hustler had been hustled. As King bagged the official purse, Riggs just had enough breath left to gasp 'the girl was all over me; I didn't realize she was so quick.'

Bobby certainly looked done but the artful old dodger was no fool. He covered his losses by endorsement and rights deals and eventually took home three times what his conqueror received. Needless to say, the Pasadena suicide bridge saw none of the promised action.

The result proved only than one 29-year-old female champ could beat one male 55-year-old ex-champ, but it did much to give women's tennis the platform it deserved and to take the whole game into the showbiz age.

As for Bobby, he carried on hustling right to the end. In 1985, aged 67, he teamed up with Vitas Gerulaitis to challenge Martina Navratilova and Pam Shriver. Once again, the women triumphed.

In a lifetime of strange games Riggs did seemingly everything from playing Gardnar Mulloy on ice in 1953 to inflicting the most weird handicaps on himself to make the odd buck or two. When he played in fishing gear complete with waders, basket round his neck and a landing net in his left hand he looked an odd sight.

But scarcely any odder than when he played an entire match with a lion cub on a lead in constant tow. Playing three-legged tennis strapped to a colleague was a mere breeze after that.

Even Riggs's choice of venues for his novelty matches was seldom ordinary; most were played on the courts of the Tennis Center in mid-Manhattan which just happened to be on the roof of a 13-storey skyscraper.

When Riggs died on 25 October 1995 the tennis world lost a great champion and true eccentric, but he will always be remembered for ultimately losing the Battle of the Sexes in the most hyped tennis match of all time.

A DEUCE OF AN EFFORT

SURBITON, MAY 1975

Surbiton has never been noted for its excesses but try telling that to Keith Glass, one of Surrey County's finest lawn tennis players.

If he'd needed someone to vent his frustration on after his experience in the first round of the Surrey Grasscourt Championships of 1975, maybe he should have sought out a Frenchman for it was the French who gave us the term 'deuce'.

Back in the sixteenth century when a player fought back to 40–all, they reasoned he'd earned the chance not to be beaten on the very next point: '*À deux*', they cried democratically, literally 'to two'.

'I have a *deuce*,' paraphrased the ever linguistically challenged English tennis player as he hung on in there at 40--all with all the Tudor tenacity he could muster.

Therein lay the genesis of Keith Glass's least favourite tennis score.

Surbiton wasn't a Wimbledon but it was a prestige tournament in the British tennis calendar and well worth winning. Keith Glass set his initial sights simply on getting past the first round. In his way on Monday 26 May stood a best-of-three-sets contest against Rhodesian A. G. Fawcett.

What a first-set battle it was. Glass fought back from 5–3 down to 5–all and refused to yield. At 8-all they entered a tie-break, still just a four-year-old infant in the British game. Glass conquered the new-fangled scoring oddity to canter through it 7–2 and take the set 9–8. British nerve had been tested and found to be steady.

So to the second set and his encounter with an old-fangled scoring system he would never forget. Trailing at 3–1, Glass sensed that Tony Fawcett was upping his game ready to close out. Now was the time for the British player again to show some spirit.

The score reached deuce. Advantage Fawcett. Deuce. Advantage Glass. Deuce. Advantage Glass. Deuce. Limitations on the thickness of this book prevent me from giving the full sequence. All in all the umpire called 'deuce' 37 times in that fifth game of the second set, a game of fully 80 points which entered the record books for the most points in a single game ever officially recorded. It lasted 31 minutes.

If you expect me to say Glass lost it, then think again. British resolve triumphed once more as he finally heard those blissful words 'Game to Glass'.

Now just 3–2 down he resolved to continue his supreme effort but the body and concentration failed him.

Having already played enough points to have won the entire match Glass, as it were, was shattered. He won only one more game in the second set and wimped out with a feeble two in the third as Tony Fawcett upheld Rhodesian pride with an 8–9, 6–3, 6–2 victory.

Keith Glass may have lost the match but everyone agreed he'd made a deuce of an effort.

ARTHUR KEEPS COOL

LAGOS, NIGERIA, FEBRUARY 1976

If ever you've wondered what tennis players do when they're not playing in the sophisticated surroundings of a Grand Slam, read on.

Because it's their job, they not surprisingly play tennis, and that means travelling to play in some tournaments in which resilience beyond the call of duty comes in useful. Just ask Arthur Ashe.

As the first black American to win Wimbledon and the first ever winner, in 1968, of the American Open, his legendary name was always one to champion good causes. Having made pioneering tours of Africa in 1970 and 1971, in which he discovered an 11-year-old future star by the name of Yannick Noah, he'd always fancied going back in a bigger way. He knew that Africa had 'potential'.

So in 1976 he was delighted to spearhead a World Championship Tennis tour to Nigeria which gave Black Africa its first big-time professional tournament.

The welcome party in Lagos on Wednesday went well. And, when Ashe beat the Australian Dick Crealy four days later, one press report said that 'he cruised to a 6–2, 6–1 win in 40 relaxed minutes'.

But any thoughts that the trip to Africa had simply been a jolly are quickly dispelled by accounts of what happened between times.

The tennis on day one was fine although the spirits of some

of the players were dampened by the accommodation. The magnificent sounding Embassy Palace Hotel turned out to be a converted army camp.

Day two, Friday the thirteenth. They might have known. The military theme continued as a group calling themselves the 'Young Revolutionary Officers' staged an attempted coup. It was 'Revolution Stop Play' as not a ball was hit.

Trying to keep cool, two players were advised by rifle-toting guards to 'kindly leave the swimming pool' while the New Zealand embassy were informed that their star player Brian Fairlie had had his passport confiscated and was under house arrest.

As revolutions go, though, this one was a bit of a farce, as Fairlie was in fact enjoying a game of squash at the time, blissfully unaware of his strategic role in an international incident.

Arthur Ashe, meanwhile, maintaining customary medita-tory calm, continued with a Spanish lesson as demands were made by the rebel forces.

'I do not agree with this revolution,' responded a high-up general.

And that was that. The easiest quelling of all time. But any thoughts of getting back to tennis the next day were just as quickly quashed.

As 14 February dawned the players might well have feared a St Valentine's Day Massacre but what they got was a government declaration of a state of national mourning for the regrettable events of the previous day. Once again the tennis bit the dust.

Being able to play on the Sunday was a great relief although the atmosphere was far from strawberries and cream.

The temperature was 120 degrees Fahrenheit with a humidity quotient of 80 per cent. The US ambassador was treated to an armed guard but unfortunately the canopy over his seat in the royal box (concrete terrace) had collapsed that morning after a heavy rainstorm.

It was soggy on court too as, in one corner, water had seeped up between the rubber carpet and the concrete underneath.

181

But Arthur Robert Ashe, lost to tennis so tragically prematurely in 1993 aged only 49, took a deep breath and remembered his ambassadorial responsibilities. Keeping his head when all around were losing theirs, he played and won in this most bizarre of tournaments in the serene fashion he made his own.

So now you know what tennis players do when they're not playing Grand Slams.

HOUSTON WE HAVE A PROBLEM

FORO ITALICO, ROME, MAY 1976

How many times have we heard players complain after losing that a break for rain or bad light was responsible for disturbing their concentration?

It's an old chestnut that's rescued many who've blown their chances. Maybe the muscles stiffen or that time in the dressing room allows self-doubt to creep in or an opponent to muster new strength and confidence.

Poppycock it may be in nine cases out of ten but if ever anyone did have a genuine case for bemoaning a break in play it must be the Australian pairing John Newcombe and Geoff Masters. At Rome's famous Foro Italico on 30 May 1976 they faced the American Brian Gottfried and his partner Raul Ramirez of Mexico in the final of the men's doubles at the Italian Championships.

The Aussies lost the first set 7–6 after a tie-break, bounced back to take the second 7–5 but then slipped to 6–3 in the third. Gottfried and Ramirez had taken the title in 1974 and 1975 but Masters and Newcombe were determined to stop the hat trick and promptly took the fourth 6–3 to level at 2 sets all.

It was then that that whimsical intruder 'bad light', just as mischievous in sunny Italy as at its spiritual home Wimbledon, decided to put paid to play for the day. When the match later recommenced Gottfried and Ramirez prevailed 6–3 to take their third title.

Did the Australians have a bad night's sleep? As it happens, that wasn't an excuse they needed, for such were the working commitments of each of the four players that it was fully 108 days before the match restarted.

So when the umpire called 'play' on 15 September he ended the longest break for bad light ever recorded.

Masters and Newcombe might also have claimed a certain degree of disorientation when they finally walked back on court. None of the surroundings looked familiar, nor were the faces in the crowd classically Italian. That might have been because the Italian organizing committee had reacted to the crisis in a positive, if unusual, manner: 'Houston we have a problem,' they cried, and Houston responded in positive manner. Thus it was that Masters and Newcombe lost the final in Texas, USA, not in Italy.

Having travelled thousands of miles and played thousands of paints in the meantime, who wouldn't be put out? Gottfried and Ramirez, that's who – Houston, Rome, May, September – it was all the same to them.

John Newcombe, in particular, was entitled to wonder what was going on in 1976 because it wasn't the first two-centre match he'd been asked to play. From 28 February to 2 March in Brisbane, Australia, he'd won a singles and a doubles playing Davis Cup against New Zealand only for the tie to be washed out by a cyclone at 2 rubbers all. Three and a half months later, on Saturday 19 June, Newcombe played the deciding singles against Brian Fairlie, again under rain-laden skies, but this time in Nottingham, England. On that occasion he clinched the tie with an 8–6, 5–7, 11–9, 6–3 victory.

Players have often complained that they travel so much they don't know where they are from one match to the next. John Newcombe's diary for 1976 rather proves the point.

A CASE OF DÉJÀ VU

ROLAND GARROS, PARIS, JUNE 1976

All the locals were happy when Madame J. Lovera won the
women's doubles with her partner Florella Bonicelli at the
1976 French Open: 'Such a fine French player,' they cooed
with Gallic pride after the 6–4, 1–6, 6–3 victory over the
American Miss Harter and her German partner Mrs Masthof.

Those regulars at the Roland Garros Stadium who liked to
compare the new champions with those of yesteryear were
soon debating the merits of Madame Lovera.

Her style, some said, was 'very reminiscent of the blonde
girl Mme J. B. Chanfreau' who'd won the same title with
everybody's French favourite, Françoise Durr, back in 1971
and 1970.

Some whose memories went back even further begged to
differ. Mme Lovera was 'much more like the young Australian
girl Gail Sherriff' who'd won with Françoise Durr in 1967,
they insisted.

'But older. Yes, definitely older,' someone chipped in.

The debate need not have raged for long, for if they'd read
their programmes instead of looking at the scoreboard they'd
soon have realized that their 'French' heroine Mme J. Lovera
was one and the same as Mme J. B. Chanfreau who in turn was
one and the same as the gutsy Australian youngster Miss Gail
Sherriff.

Believe it or not, lady tennis players do get married and
sometimes more than once. And these fussy umpires will

185

insist on using married names and even hubby's initials.

Remember Mrs R. A. Cawley? Evonne Goolagong. What about Mrs J. M. Lloyd? Chris Evert, of course. All very confusing if you're not up to press with who's married who.

And it's all such a lottery what name you end up with. Plain old Margaret Smith must surely have been pleased with the fortuitous tennis connection when she became Margaret Court in 1967. Mrs Slocock, meanwhile, was doubtless mighty relieved back in 1908 to pair off with the much safer Roderick McNair.

But what of Mrs Nutcombe-Quick back in the early years of the twentieth century? Was her new title really any better than her maiden name, Miss Batty Bellew? Perhaps that's why she married a second time to rid herself of the Nutcombe-Quick tag. If so, she made an almighty blunder: 'Advantage Mrs Crundell-Punnett' just doesn't have that ring of star quality that champions need.

She certainly didn't perform as well as Gail Sherriff, whose record of winning the French Open doubles four times under three different identities should confuse the statisticians of the future for many years to come.

HERE'S THE WORLD'S MOST FAMOUS PLAYER

SANTA ROSA, CALIFORNIA, JUNE 1976

How can one possibly decide the world's most famous player of all time? Bill Tilden, Suzanne Lenglen, John McEnroe, Billie Jean King, Bjorn Borg, Martina Navratilova, Pete Sampras, Martina Hingis?

They and many others all have a claim. But there is one challenger that might well have been overlooked, and he probably has the best claim of all.

Born on 2 October 1950 he is still going strong. Untold millions follow his progress. His nervous mannerisms and cheesy grin endear him to his adoring fans.

He has, too, a great repertoire of one-liners. When he was interviewed by Charles Brown after a vigorous match under the Santa Rosa sun in June 1976 it went like this:

'I hear you're thinking of playing at Wimbledon this month.'

'I might. I have to find out more details. I wonder if you have to bring along a can of balls.'

Off court he is an accomplished novel writer and daring pilot. A number of books have charted his full tennis career and in 1975 he published his own work entitled *How To Get Away With Eleven Bad Calls In a Row*.

Despite his experience he has never won a major tournament as he has been dogged constantly by a sense of insecurity. Back in the spring of 1975, again considering

187

Wimbledon, he was asked how he'd feel playing Ashe, Connors, Borg or Okker. The reply was revealing: 'I hate playing guys like that. They keep hitting the ball back.'

It is both that inner self-doubt and a somewhat intolerant temper that has always stopped him playing doubles. Ask him about that and he will say: 'I only play singles. The only time I ever played doubles was a mixed with the garage door.' Then he adds tartly: 'We lost. I played very well but the garage choked.'

Despite never truly hitting his peak, the player the public love to love (especially the ladies) has had more exposure than anyone in the game and he was even featured in a Broadway musical.

It's the press, though, that have really given him the mass exposure he enjoys. USA, Europe, Australia, Asia, Africa – pick any one of 2,800 newspapers worldwide and there's a fair chance that each and every day this superstar of the modern game will have featured.

And this diminutive character hasn't finished yet despite passing his fiftieth birthday.

So who is the guy beneath the famous eyeshade? He is the most instantly recognizable of all tennis stars. He is Snoopy the beagle, not just the self-proclaimed world's best tennis player, but the world's best known dog too. Lassie, Fred Basset and Rin Tin Tin were all very well but they never played tennis.

Despite being underdog and usually losing to his regular opponent, the bird-brained Woodstock, Snoopy continues to hit now and then in the Peanuts strip cartoon in which he stars and probing interviewer Charlie Brown still fires the questions.

Sadly, Snoopy lost his 77-year-old coach and creator Charles Schulz on 12 February 2000 and his appearances are now more limited, but his legion of fans remain loyal.

The beagle with attitude is still proving what those on the tennis circuit have known for years. It's dog eat dog out there.

AN UNHOLY MESS

NEWPORT BEACH, CALIFORNIA, APRIL 1977

Newport Beach, California, just south of Los Angeles, is a long way from the English lawns upon which tennis was first played. Perhaps that's appropriate, as if ever there was an occasion when the vicarage garden party image of the game was irrevocably laid to rest it was at this West Coast resort on Sunday 17 April 1977.

This is the tale of the minister of the Church, the oil slick, the racket attack and the mass demonstration. It doesn't sound like an everyday story of ordinary tennis folk but then it's not every day that the United States plays South Africa in the Davis Cup at the height of the apartheid debate. The tension had been mounting for over a decade.

The serious side to this strange affair had been a major problem for years. Official United Nations policy was to strongly discourage all sporting contact with 'racist South African sports bodies', but many nations purportedly 'put sport above politics' and played on. Anti-apartheid activists said that such blind-eye attitudes simply condoned racism and there had been trouble almost everywhere South African representatives played, not simply directed against them but their hosts as well.

In 1968 the Sweden *v.* Rhodesia tie in Bastad had to be moved to Bandol in the South of France as a 1,500-strong rioting mob, some armed with iron bars, lumps of concrete and bottles, made play impossible.

A year later, but rather gentler, it was Great Britain's turn as bags of flour hurtled over the stands to bomb the court at the Redlands Club in Bristol. Other nations, meanwhile, did refuse to play, none more nobly than India who passed up the chance of glory by declining to face South Africa in the 1974 final.

'Dwight Davis must have turned in his grave,' said *Lawn Tennis* magazine of the man who founded the competition back in 1900 in the spirit of friendly national rivalry. Hence the enhanced significance when South Africa travelled to 'white supremacist' United States in 1977.

Trouble they expected and trouble they got. Seven hundred demonstrators constantly chanted 'South Africa go home' outside the court arena but both sides refused to be deterred from simply playing tennis. Police ejected early court invaders and amongst the real fans a spirit of 'the match must go on' began to build.

It was after America had built a 2 rubbers to 0 lead that a church minister decided on more direct action. Home pairing Stan Smith and Bob Lutz were already 2 sets to 0 ahead against Frew McMillan and Byron Bertram when 29-year-old black activist Reverend Roland Dortsch rushed wildly on to the United States end of the court and emptied a plastic bottle of motor oil over the green surface. His colleague Deacon Alexander had his own bottle snatched before he could add to the spreading slick.

But as the American party saw red, the Reverend got more than he bargained for. Team captain Tony Trabert, heroic veteran of many Davis Cup matches during the much calmer 1950s, flailed at him with a racket backed by the cheering 6,000 crowd.

It took 41 minutes to clean the court and just a little longer for America to clinch the tie with a 7–5, 6–1, 3–6, 6–3 victory. 'UNITED STATES CLEAN UP,' said *The Times*.

Scenes very foreign to the game of lawn tennis they certainly were but Trabert was unrepentant: 'I brought a good old graphite racket along as a weapon and just hit them a couple of times,' he explained later.

The South African captain backed him all the way: 'I was very happy with the genuine crowd and the police have been wonderful,' he told reporters. 'What Trabert did to the court invaders really makes you feel good.'

Strange demonstrations, strange retaliations and strange reactions. Who could blame Dwight Davis if he's still turning today?

DOCTORED!

FOREST HILLS, NEW YORK, SEPTEMBER 1977

'Whatever else it may be it is not, as Virginia Wade suggests, "just another match".' That was how the *Guardian* previewed the first-round game in the ladies' singles at the 1977 US Open between Britain's Virginia Wade and Dr Renée Richards of the United States.

What made the pressmen so sure that such an apparently ordinary match would in fact go down in history as arguably the most extraordinary of all time? The word is one that was surely never used in the world of Victorian tennis – chromosomes.

The story starts in New York on 19 September 1934 with the birth of a bouncing baby boy, Richard Raskind. Dick grew up to be a strapping lad of 6 feet 2 inches, captained his Yale University team in 1954 and developed into one of the leading amateurs on America's East Coast circuit. He was good enough to play in the US Nationals at Forest Hills in 1960 but not nearly good enough to overcome the reigning Wimbledon champion and defending US title holder Neale Fraser. The Australian beat him 6–0, 6–1, 6–1 in the first round.

Those sort of results weren't too disastrous for Raskind, though, as he forged another career as a leading opthalmologist, got married and fathered a son.

The tale takes its next turn in La Jolla, California, in July 1976, when an amateur ladies' tournament was won there in fine style by another doctor, Renée Clark. Her 6–1, 6–1 victory over Robin Harris was pretty impressive and accomplished with the sort of power that might only be generated by someone with her muscular frame and conspicuous height advantage.

It didn't take long for an old acquaintance to put two and two together, nor for the proverbial to hit the fan once the news was out. Renée Clark wasn't really Renée Clark. She was Renée Richards. What's more, Renée Richards was really Richard Raskind. The 'he' had turned into a 'she' and the new life and identity she had hoped to take up 3,000 miles from home were blown wide open.

Back in August 1975 when the op was done they called it a sex change. Now it's gender reassignment surgery, but no matter what the label it hadn't happened in tennis before and it set everyone all of a flutter. The press, naturally, had a field day.

Some female players refused to play against Ms Richards. Others argued about whether they felt comfortable sharing a locker room and shower with her. The tennis authorities, meanwhile, banned her from competing in major championships for women unless she could pass a chromosome test, which was medically impossible.

Richards fought her corner and the whole affair turned into a Human Rights issue and media circus with huge ramifications well beyond the world of sport. When a New York judge finally ruled that Richards could be regarded in law as a woman, her right to enter the 1977 US Open was confirmed.

And there the circle completes itself, albeit in rather unspectacular fashion. For the truth was that, whether male or female, the 42-year-old opthalmologist who took on Wimbledon champion Virginia Wade on Thursday 2 September 1977, was no better a tennis player than 'she' had been 17 years previously at the same venue when Neale Fraser had seen 'him' off. Virginia Wade duly did the business in the goldfish bowl atmosphere of the Stadium Court, running out an easy winner 6–1, 6–4.

The *Guardian* put it in a nutshell: 'Those who feared a freak show,' they reported, 'had worried unduly. It was a dignified and rather unspectacular encounter in which Dr Richards's immobility found her out. It was all over in an hour.'

Richards later became coach to Martina Navratilova before returning to her life in medicine as director of opthalmology at the Manhattan Eye Clinic in New York. Her story was sufficiently notorious to inspire a TV movie with Vanessa Redgrave in the lead role.

Few, if any, tennis episodes could be stranger – to play in both the men's and women's singles in the US Championships takes some beating and only one person (or should we say two?) has done it so far.

COMPUTER LINESMEN

EDINBURGH, SEPTEMBER 1977

It was the headline the players had all been waiting for.
'COMPUTERS INSTEAD OF LINESMEN' it read. And it wasn't April Fool's Day or sensationalist tabloid hokum; this was *The Times*: 'A computer-controlled line-call system will be used in competitive tennis for the first time,' it announced, 'when the international indoor circuit sponsored by Pernod begins its series in Edinburgh on Monday 26 September.'

An electronic system was first used in Dallas on the glitzy World Championship Tennis circuit in 1974, but that was only a service-line bleeper. Edinburgh would get the full monty.

And this was no mad professor's wild fancy. This was the invention of Dr David Subran, a real scientist who'd taken seven years to perfect his 'Subcall' system in conjunction with Slazengers, whose specially designed balls would make the whole thing foolproof.

The 'doc' spared no detail in explaining the system to the press: 'Flat-woven ribbon cables are attached to all the white lines and the new treated fabric on the balls acts as a conductor so when the ball lands fractionally outside the line an electrical circuit is completed which in turn is connected to a computer.'

From there it was child's play. A light would appear on the umpire's control panel backed by an audible bleep: 'Marketing plans are well advanced,' purred Dr Subran, 'with retail prices at around £6,000 and lots of interest being shown.'

It seemed a straightforward case of 'today Edinburgh,

tomorrow the world'. The inventor, no doubt, was already planning a series of exotic vacations.

But this strange yarn is as much a tale of two headlines as the demise of linesmen. When play got under way at the indoor Meadowbank Centre doubts began to emerge. Players raised eyebrows as balls looking 'good' produced bleeps and those obviously out were met with absolute silence.

Britain's Mark Cox saw off Nigel Sears 6–1, 6–1 but admitted diplomatically 'I was never quite certain the system was working.' David Lloyd and some of the other players were rather more vociferous in their observations and *The Times* headline of 29 September must have brought David Subran out in a cold sweat: 'SHORT CIRCUIT IN THE ELECTRONIC LINESMAN.'

After just three days' play the system had been withdrawn: 'Unfortunately the players have been dragging their feet across the tape and drawing the cables together. I'm afraid it's back to the drawing board,' explained tournament director George Hendon.

Technologically speaking one must admit that 1977 is virtually prehistory so the more recent postscript to this valiant effort will of course read rather differently. Fast-forward to the 1993 US Open.

The United States Tennis Association knew they'd got it right. After all, they'd spent $75,000 installing the Australian Tennis Electronic Line (TEL) system at Flushing Meadows. It was, they were told, 'accurate to within a millimetre'.

USTA director Jay Snyder allayed the fears of the sceptics by explaining that there'd been 'two years of intense testing' and that 'the technology is similar to that used in guided missiles'.

A quick dress rehearsal in the qualifying tournament at the end of August would precede the grand unveiling in the championship proper.

You've guessed it! TEL became confused, reacting to a player's ankle bracelet and picking up the metal eyelets in tennis shoes.

'Consistent malfunction' was the official line as the plug

was pulled on TEL just 72 hours before the start of the US Open.

So what's the update as we go to press? Not surprisingly, matters have moved on in the twenty-first century. The latest equipment makes instantaneous audible and visible signals as its pivotal twin optical detectors relay signals to a complex computer. The user-friendly machine is able to move up and down or side to side on articulated legs to ensure an unrestricted line view at all times. Costs, moreover, are minimal and the system has been described as the best ever in tennis history.

It is called *homo sapiens* and thrives on an occasional cup of tea.

AGE SHALL NOT WEARY THEM

CHARLOTTESVILLE, VIRGINIA, SEPTEMBER 1977

For most men of advancing years a visit to the Boar's Head promises a quiet pint of foaming ale, a pensioner's special roast lunch or, for those still active in sports, a vigorous game of dominoes or cribbage.

But not so those who wended their way to the Boar's Head Sports Club in Charlottesville, Virginia, in the late summer of 1977. They were intent on making tennis history.

As president of the Super Senior Tennis Association, C. Alphonso Smith was one of those men who saw age as no barrier to sporting prowess. But although seniors tournaments (never ever call them veterans as it upsets them) had been played before, there had never been an official national championship for those of octogenarian status.

Being a man of action, Smith didn't whinge about it into his beer, he simply beetled off down to The Boar's Head and organized the tournament.

The club had already entered the record books once. Back in 1973 they'd organized a juvenile tournament of sorts, for youngsters of 75 years and over. But in 1977 it was the big boys' turn, qualification for entry being a birth certificate dated 1897 or earlier.

Being played on clay, exhausting long rallies, throbbing bunions and scuffed knees might have been expected, but that didn't worry the two singles finalists who met on 25 September. And it was top seed John L. Giegrich from

198

Jamesburg, New Jersey, who saw off second seed Henry Doyle from Little Rock, Arkansas, in what *Tennis USA* magazine described as 'a hard three-set match, 6–3, 3–6, 6–4'.

While the white-haired, golden tanned and bespectacled Giegrich celebrated his triumph, which was not, as far as we can be aware, preceded by a jubilant leap over the net, Doyle might have been forgiven for retreating to the club house for a soothing linament rub, warming drink and an early night: 'Hey, you've got to be kidding buddy,' Doyle fires, 'I've got a doubles to play and some revenge to take.'

No problems there, as Doyle teamed up with Eldon Roark from Memphis, Tennessee, to take the USTA over 80 national doubles title. This time it was Giegrich and his partner Jake Pettus, all the way from Austin, Texas, who lost out in another 'hard three-setter' 1–6, 6–4, 7–5.

Maybe Doyle was overcome with emotion, or simply prostrate on the locker-room floor, but he left his partner Eldon Roark to give the interviews to *Tennis USA*: 'It took me over 65 years of sweat and toil on the courts to get somewhere, but it has finally paid off. Shows it pays to be stubborn,' he said.

On the question of sponsorship he was upbeat: 'I'm an optimist. Maybe offers will come. We'll be very reasonable. As 80-year-old champs we'll settle for 80 per cent of what Connors and Borg are getting for endorsements, and we'll consider anything; rackets, shorts, long-johns, false teeth, laxatives, bedroom slippers, anything except gardening tools – we positively will not endorse such harmful boring devices. We need the money but we have our principles.'

The speed might not be what it was, but for dogged determination and self-deprecation these oldsters surely beat the young superstars hands down.

This age business is, of course, all relative. The 'Bounding Basque' Jean Borotra, a legend in the 1920s and 1930s, simply refused to give up playing. Every year he would turn out at Queen's Club for the International Club of France in their annual fixture against their British counterparts, and he played his last match there as a still sprightly 93-year-old.

A Swedish gentleman, too, was once famously photographed enjoying a game on his one hundred and fifth birthday. Rumours that he wore a tennis shirt emblazoned with the slogan 'Do I come here often?' are unsubstantiated. I forget his name, but then again so did he.

Joking apart, those who play seniors' tennis are a real credit to the game and themselves – long may they continue.

DIVINE INTERVENTION

STOCKHOLM, NOVEMBER 1977

Anyone who said American Sandy Mayer hadn't got a prayer of winning the Stockholm Open on the superfast tiled indoor court at the Swedish capital's famous Kungli Hallen was missing the point, because that's precisely what he did have.

The 25-year-old New Yorker wasn't expected to win Stockholm, one of the most coveted indoor titles, and he'd been playing in the circus atmosphere of World Team Tennis back in the States all through the summer, arguably not the best preparation for serious competition.

But as the *Guardian* reported, his progress to the final seemed supercharged: 'He exploded through a strong field,' they wrote, 'never appearing in real danger of losing a set as he overwhelmed Brian Gottfried, Harold Solomon and Stan Smith with the crushing power of his orthodox serve and volley game.'

But Mayer knew that his game wasn't quite as orthodox as some were suggesting for he had a secret weapon in his armoury. As a dedicated Fundamentalist Christian he'd been using the power of prayer to prepare for all his matches and as he'd yet to drop a set someone up there must have been on his side.

For the final against South Africa's Ray Moore on 13 November he decided to go for it in a big way. It was, after all, a Sunday. For fully 15 minutes before the match he prayed to God. No one knows what he asked for but something must

201

have worked for the match reports confirmed that 'Moore could do little to counter Mayer's blistering returns and brilliant serving.' The American won a one-sided contest 6–2, 6–4.

It doesn't work with everyone, of course. You have to be able to play a bit to start with but Mayer certainly derived comfort from his unorthodox tactics: 'I go out there and do my best,' he said after lifting the trophy, 'but whatever happens is the Lord's will.'

Mayer is by no means the only player to have received coaching of the divine kind.

The prodigious American Michael Chang once gave a post-match interview after a famous victory in which he refused to take any credit: 'It was a beautiful day for tennis and the Lord just took over,' he explained.

Sandy Mayer *v.* Michael Chang in a major final might well have been an interesting affair. Maybe that's why the supreme seeding committee made sure they were born twenty years apart.

A CAGEY GAME

COBHAM, SURREY, FEBRUARY 1978

If there is one piece of advice that sports entrepreneurs relish ignoring it's that old chestnut 'If it ain't broke don't fix it.' And it seems it's the Americans who love to tinker more than anyone.

Lawn tennis had had its ups and downs but it had been trotting along quite nicely for a hundred years, thank you very much, when the guys across the pond decided Britain just couldn't survive without Platform Tennis.

Thus it was that the first British Championships took place on Saturday 4 February 1978 at Silvermere Golf and Country Club near Cobham, Surrey.

Having apparently been at it ever since its invention in 1928, the Americans already knew the ropes and provided most of the entry. All the big world names were there. Rhodesian Hank Irvine headed the men's field and Hilary Hilton and Louise Gengler, Stan Smith's sister-in-law no less, led the female challenge. You remember them of course.

That most British institution the *Sunday Times* was just a trifle dubious: 'A whole new game has crossed the Atlantic,' it announced, 'but platform tennis could encounter rigid British resistance when us islanders see what strange things have happened to the familiar game we know.

So what hideous mutant did 'us islanders' actually witness back in February 1978? Respected tennis journalist Rex Bellamy suffered the indignity of witnessing a game:

The Americans have taken a tennis court and compressed it into a quarter of its area. They have then stuck it into a 12 foot high 'cage' of rigid wire mesh walls off which the ball may be played as in squash. The markings and scoring are the same as tennis although only one serve is allowed. Each of the four players is given a glorified table tennis bat which, though small, is 4 ounces heavier than a tennis racket and causes the extremely bouncy and brightly coloured rubber ball to whizz off it.

Seeking to counter this hint of scepticism were the promoters: 'We have 100,000 players in the States,' they hyped, 'with an active circuit and a Championship at Forest Hills which has attracted 14,000 spectators.'

Mr Bellamy, speaking for us islanders, summed up his case with a final withering damnation.

'The whole unholy hybrid,' he spluttered, 'is then raised seven feet above the ground so that the four enclosed players are like caged budgerigars on a stage.'

Lest the jury was split, he finished with a *coup de grâce* which exposed this vile impostor of a game in the worst terms possible: 'Platform tennis,' he concluded acidly, 'is played in casual clothes.'

Who said the 1970s were liberated? It might have been the 1870s as far as *The Times* readers were concerned. It goes without saying that since its debut performance Platform Tennis seems to have gone somewhat underground.

Did someone say 'underground tennis'? Now there *is* a swell idea!

ALL A MATTER OF TIMING

WIMBLEDON , JULY 1979

'Play will commence at two o'clock precisely.' That clipped announcement which invariably accompanied the Order of Play schedules in the press seemed just as much a part of Wimbledon tradition as strawberries and cream. It seemed to signify the run-like-clockwork organization of the Championships and was, of course, particularly important on finals days.

But, like all traditions, it had to come a cropper one day and, in 1979 on Saturday 7 July, the Wimbledon committee discovered that, even in SW19, nothing is sacred.

Never let it be thought that Wimbledon doesn't move with the times, though. In fact the record of the Championships has always been one of constant innovation. When colour television transmissions of the tournament began in 1968 they embraced the technology completely and now, in 1979, coverage had developed so rapidly that a live transmission of the men's finals was to go by satellite to the United States at precisely 9 am Eastern Daylight Time with millions of Americans tuning into the first ever 'Breakfast at Wimbledon' programme, set to become a veritable institution over the years ahead.

Wimbledon weren't going to be caught napping, that's for sure. Their official records proudly state: 'In 1979 new clocks were provided throughout the premises and grounds. Centre Court and No. 1 Court scoreboards were fitted with digital clocks and umpires were issued with stop watches to ensure players did not exceed the time limit between change of ends.'

Having gone to so much trouble on the chronometric front it was no surprise that Wimbledon officials gave rather short shrift to an unprecedented request from America's NBC Television Network. NBC were, naturally, keen to screen every single ball of the final between their own Roscoe Tanner and Sweden's Bjorn Borg. But it seems, what with adverts, title sequences and satellite links, a start of 2.05 pm precisely would suit the American audience rather better than the traditional 2 pm.

Would Wimbledon oblige? You've got to be joking. They might as well have asked for a nude dance troupe to call the lines.

But American TV is a powerful force. All it took was a quick chat with Roscoe and a flick through the rule book and the dastardly deed was done.

As the digital clocks showed 2 pm precisely, Mr Tanner, evidently suffering from an attack of nerves, excused himself for a bathroom break. It took him precisely five minutes to do the business and the Wimbledon men's final of 1979 duly commenced at 2.05 pm precisely. It was the ultimate *fait accompli*.

NBC executives congratulated themselves heartily. American TV viewers enjoyed their Toastie-Pops without missing a ball. The Wimbledon hierarchy was not amused.

In the face of such sacrilegious behaviour it is heartening to report that justice was done. Bjorn Borg displayed his customarily impeccable timing to win his fourth successive Wimbledon title by beating Roscoe Tanner in a five-set classic 6–7, 6–1, 3–6, 6–3, 6–4. It lasted 2 hours 49 minutes – precisely.

PASSING ON THE RECORD

WIMBLEDON, JULY 1979

Saturday 7 July 1979 is a date that still sits proudly in the record books for the legendary Californian Billie Jean King, for it was the day she clinched her twentieth Wimbledon title, a feat which even the most recent legend of the ladies' game, Martina Navratilova, has been unable to match despite repeated 'final' efforts to advance beyond 19.

Ironically enough it was the then 22-year-old Navratilova who helped King clinch the record that day when they paired to win the ladies' doubles against Betty Stove and Wendy Turnbull in a 5–7, 6–3, 6–2 victory.

Remarkable as the feat was, the match would struggle to gain admission to the gallery of strangeness but for the events off-court which surrounded it. From there we enter the world of the positively spooky.

It was another Californian, Elizabeth 'Bunny' Ryan, whose record 19 Wimbledon titles King had been trying to pass ever since she equalled it with her singles win over Evonne Goolagong in 1975. But try as she might the record eluded her as she drew a blank in 1976, 1977 and 1978, and at age 35 it seemed it might never happen.

Elizabeth Ryan had looked on rather quizzically as each attempt failed. This gutsy grand old lady of the court, once a veritable Amazon but then well into her eighties, had confined to friends that she hoped to take the record to her grave. It was that sort of winning attitude (and a rather good regular partner by the name of Suzanne Lenglen) that had brought her the record, all comprising doubles wins, between 1914 and 1934. But it was Lenglen too who generally baulked her in the singles, earning Miss Ryan, with her robust approach and famous forehand chop, the title of 'the best player never to win a Wimbledon singles'.

As each year passed, Miss Elizabeth Monatague Ryan, born 1892, became quietly convinced that she would never be surpassed. Living in London she was sprightly enough to get to Wimbledon, her spiritual home, whenever she fancied. She was there on Friday 6 July just 24 hours before her record fell, but she wasn't there the next day to see Billie Jean make history.

The headline in the *Guardian* simply read 'A CHAMPION CHAMPION TO THE END'. For, while walking around the grounds of the All England Club during her Friday visit, the 87-year-old champion collapsed from a heart attack and died in the ambulance before reaching hospital. She had first fallen ill while watching the antics of McEnroe and Fleming during the men's doubles final, although there was nothing in their rather modern behaviour to establish cause and effect.

In the *Guardian* obituary David Gray, secretary of the International Tennis Federation, captured the mood succinctly: 'Miss Ryan died,' he wrote, 'as she had played – determined not to be beaten.'

Her niece Miss Elizabeth Partridge, meanwhile, gave a gutsy reaction: 'I'm glad she didn't live to see Mrs King's win. It's good that it's happened this way. It's much better for my aunt that way.'

There is never a good time to call it a day but Elizabeth Ryan's sense of timing was certainly uncanny as the record 'passed on' in the strangest way possible.

AN UNEXPECTED EXIT

FLUSHING MEADOWS, NEW YORK, SEPTEMBER 1979

It's Friday 30 August 1979, a steamy night in New York.

They're playing under the glare of the floodlights. It's the second round of the US Open and an advertisement in the *New York Post* has just urged fans to 'Come see the fight of the century.'

It wasn't as if lively local boy John McEnroe and raging Romanian Ilie Nastase needed the tension hyping for this one. They were quite capable of causing mayhem unaided.

Brilliantly innovative as he was as a tennis player, Nastase's foul language, vile temper and petulantly childish antics were really wearing thin with the authorities. Some even doubted his sanity.

McEnroe, meanwhile, was building up a legendary repertoire of uncontrolled explosions and withering one-liners all his own.

Trouble seemed virtually guaranteed. Maybe even the first ever default from a Grand Slam event. But the tournament organizers weren't going to be caught with their pants down. They put tough guy Frank Hammond in the umpire's chair confident that his theatrical booming voice and personal presence would keep the players under control and avoid the ultimate scandal of a disqualification.

With both players seemingly intent on psyching each other out it was a tense affair. Inevitably there was the usual rash of queried calls and threatening looks but on this night the tension was heightened by the unusually volatile crowd which contained elements attracted by the sort of promotion usually reserved for a heavyweight boxing showdown at Madison Square Garden.

Naturally the brash New York crowd favoured McEnroe and cheered raucously when he took the first set 6–4. Nastase constantly stalled and protested, won the second set 6–4, but in the third was finally goaded into backchat with sections of the crowd. Things quickly turned ugly.

Umpire Hammond duly docked him a point, and then in the fourth set a game, with Nastase trailing at 2–1. Nastase raged even more wildly in response. Conscious of the job he'd been asked to do Hammond replied by defaulting the Romanian forthwith. 'Game, set and match McEnroe,' he boomed.

Much as they favoured McEnroe, the crowd went wild. They'd paid for tennis and that's what they wanted. Beer cans, popcorn buckets and all manner of other objects rained down on court and the catcalls and jeers became threateningly angry.

The uproar, one of the most chaotic tennis had ever witnessed, lasted 15 minutes. Tournament Referee Mike Blanchard arrived on court to lend support to Hammond. 'Nastase must go,' he said. Then came tournament director Bill Talbert followed by grand prix supervisor Frank Smith until all four officials convened on court beneath the gaze of a crowd later described by journalists as 'a howling mob'.

Both players' behaviour was far from exemplary but Nastase in particular had overstepped the mark. It was obvious someone had to go as the quartet of officials got their heads together for some fighting talk. Needless to say, marching orders were duly issued.

Strange, then, that the record books say that McEnroe won this match 6–4, 4–6, 6–3, 6–2, which oddly suggests that it ran its full course. And that's precisely because it did.

When 'game, set and match' was finally called to send the crowd home happy, it wasn't the voice of Frank Hammond they heard. Tournament director Bill Talbert had well and truly bottled it and put Mike Blanchard in the chair.

Player and crowd pressure had prevailed and in one of the oddest official decisions of all time umpire Hammond had been sent off!

The *Guardian* headline stormed 'MOB RULE WINS DAY'.

Hammond, meanwhile, was pig sick: 'I've been an official for 32 years,' he said, 'but when I was defaulted instead of Nastase I lost all faith and all heart.'

THE LOVE DOUBLES

BATTERSEA PARK, LONDON, MAY 1980

'Roll up! Roll up!' was the cry in Battersea Park on the evening of Monday 19 May 1980. And they did, as a host of celebrities decked out in evening dress filed their way into a red and white striped circus big top for one of the oddest matches ever staged.

'LOVE ALL IN BATTERSEA PARK' cooed *The Times*, and there's the clue to this sugary confection of a contest promoted under the syrupy banner of 'The Love Doubles'.

The concept was a simple one. The incomparable Swedish 'Ice Man' Bjorn Borg would partner his Romanian fiancée Mariana Simionescu in a head to head against married pairing Chris and John Lloyd, who'd just celebrated their first wedding anniversary.

By now you'll either be sighing 'Aah' or screaming 'Why?' depending on your sentimentality rating. The contest was originally arranged purely as a commercial enterprise by an American hair and beauty care company but late in the day another loving couple, Princess Anne and Captain Mark Phillips, had joined the happy throng to promote the match for charity.

With £41,000 going to the winners, £27,000 to the losers and rather less going to charity, *The Times* reported 'much wailing and gnashing of teeth amongst traditionalists' but the 2,700 who paid between £10 and £25 to be there didn't seem to mind.

Except, perhaps, those that didn't quite see all the action. Those in the cheap seats, regrettably, couldn't actually see the surface of the court because of those in the raised posh seats in front of them. They had, said a bemused reporter, 'an oddly intermittent view of the ball amidst the shifting heads, heaving shoulders and whirling arms of the two couples although it was obvious there was some action going on because the appropriate noises were emerging'.

As if that wasn't irritating enough, they'd been entertained pre-match by a fancy dress reconstruction of the first Wimbledon final followed by an interview with tennis fashion icon Teddy Tinling waxing lyrical about his designs for the wedding dresses of both couples. Unmissable entertainment of course.

Outside everything was simply perfect: 'The park was at its loveliest and amid the trees around the lake were ducks and dogs, pigeons and joggers, and a German Shepherd dog standing proudly on the prow of a lazily drifting boat,' wrote *The Times*.

One begins to wonder whether this was tongue-in-cheek reporting especially as the same paper's headline after the match was 'LOVE DOUBLES TAKE LLOYDS AN HOUR'. Was that purely a comment on their all too easy 6–4, 6–3 victory or was *The Times* daring to be risqué?

Who knows? Or do I hear 'Who cares?' Television viewers evidently did, as the match highlights next day were given Star Programme billing. Then again, the competition was *Cheggers Plays Pop* and *Ask the Family* in which 'the lovable Robert Robinson introduces the Mills family from Darlington and the Seniors from Stoke.' OK, so it's a toss up.

There is a postscript to the most artificial, squeaky clean, frothiest meringue of a tennis match ever staged but it is one that only the most cynical (not me) would suggest reflects the enduring importance of the contest in tennis history.

Both the two pairings and the royal couple have, how can we put it delicately, long since 'gone their separate ways'.

CUSHIONING THE BLOW

WIMBLEDON, JUNE 1981

As tennis fans know, there's nothing like following a real ding-dong battle all the way to the final point, especially when it involves a British player snatching victory from the jaws of defeat.

There's also nothing quite like the strange reaction of a perfectly respectable tennis fan when denied that ultimate pleasure.

The Centre Court crowd on the balmy evening of Tuesday 30 June 1981 was in fine mood as Britain's 'Devon Cream' girl Sue Barker and American Ann Kiyomura, seeded ninth, began battle with fourth seeds Jo Anne Russell and Virginia Ruzici.

But heads dropped as Barker and Kiyomura lost the first set 6–4 and trailed 5–3 in the second. The crowd, many of whom had gained belated entry to the sacred court only by dint of early leavers handing in tickets, prepared to gather belongings and troop home.

Who knows what galvanized the underdogs at that point, but galvanized they were as Barker and Kiyomura stormed back to take the second set on a tie-break.

Now it was 'game on' and the crowd settled in for the duration. Or so they thought. With the score at 5–all in the deciding set, with no tie-break to come and a fading light, the fans looked on anxiously as the referee surveyed the skies: 'We can see,' they urged the officials, but to no avail as they were denied the climax they'd waited for. Play was called off at 9.35 pm.

The British thing to do would have been to file away demurely but the crowd had gathered up a head of steam and bayed for somebody's blood. First boos and jeers rang out, then programmes and plastic cups were tossed on to court, followed by the real heavy battery of a barrage of leather Wimbledon seat cushions.

The officials later claimed vindication as next day six more games were needed for Barker and Kiyomura to take the match with a 9–7 third set cliffhanger, this time in broad daylight: 'That's what happens when the hoi polloi are let in late in the day,' some of the reactionaries were heard to mutter: 'It wouldn't have happened in our day before the war,' sniffed the old campaigners.

That is unless the day happened to be Saturday 20 July 1935, which is, so the history books assure us, before the war.

On this occasion Court No. 1 was hosting the Davis Cup inter-zone final between USA and Germany. Such was the British interest in overseas stars that wildly enthusiastic crowds gathered for the event, heightened by the fact that the winners would face the cup-holders Great Britain in the final Challenge Round a week later.

But it was disappointment all round as the rain came down after the opening match between Budge and Henkel leaving the fans waiting expectantly for the glamour singles between Wilmer Alison and Baron Gottfried Von Cramm.

Undeterred, though, they waited and waited and were finally rewarded as at six o'clock the sun broke through and shone brightly.

All looked settled, preparations were made and the covers came off. *The Times* described the crowd as 'eager, in fact noisily eager, to see the match begin'.

The problem was, no one had told the ground staff or spectators of a private arrangement the two captains had come to before the tie ever started. Because of awkward shadows and the lowering angle of sunlight that was known to afflict Court No. 1, it had been agreed that in the event of evening sunshine play would cease at 7 pm.

It fell to the hapless Wimbledon secretary Major Larcombe to announce to the enthusiastic crowd under July sunshine that 'there will be no more play today'. Not a single point of the top-billing match was played.

The place erupted. Beer bottles, books, hats and literally hundreds of cushions were hurled on court leaving it resembling a battleground. Groups of apoplectic fans demanded their money back and stormed the Davis Cup offices before finally cornering Wimbledon assistant secretary Norah Cleather on the staircase to her office. Only when the police were called did she escape. She later wrote in her autobiography that it was 'the most unpleasant Wimbledon experience I ever had'.

Evidently strangeness is a timeless quality and it seems crowd behaviour 1935-style was even worse than in 1981, which is one in the eye for the sticklers.

But then their excuse *was* a pretty good one. It was the only known case of 'Sun Stopped Play' at Wimbledon.

WHEN THE PLAYERS CALLED THE LINES

MIAMI BEACH, FLORIDA, DECEMBER 1981

If ever there was a time when the question of 'bad calls' reached fever pitch it must have been the early 1980s. Jimmy Connors, J. P. McEnroe and countless others saw to that.

Despite myriad new guidelines being issued to officials the explosions continued with nerve-shattering regularity. Electronic systems, too, had been tried and found equally wanting. Nor did the players and new technology always mix; Ilie Nastase once jumped on a magic eye and then declared, 'It isn't working.'

The position was so bad, argued some of the players, that it would be better to dispense with line judges altogether: 'Let the players call their own lines,' they cried, 'then we'll have a lot less arguing.'

Nearing a state of desperation the authorities decided to call their bluff. Christmas was as good a time to try it as any. It is, after all, the season of goodwill to all men. Thus it was that the 1981 World Junior Championships at the Orange Bowl in Miami Beach were made the subject of an experiment that would surely rid tennis of its greatest scourge for all time.

Unfortunately, airborne creatures of the porcine kind are no more common in the December Florida skies than they are anywhere else. Thus ensued this bizarre affair.

Everything was going so well in the final of the Under-18 boys' doubles on Monday 28 December. The Swedish pairing

217

Henrik Sundstrom and Magnus Tideman took the first set 7–6 after a knife-edged tie-break. America's top junior duo Matt Anger and Todd Witsken, backed by a partisan home crowd, stormed back to take the second 6–3.

Umpire Ernie Rosmarin had never had it so good. All he had to do was sit back and relax, call the scores and nod benign agreement at every line call. Barring some obligatory racket throwing the festive spirit held good and there wasn't a real dispute in sight.

Even in the deciding third set, as the Swedes edged to 5–4, there was scarcely a whimper, and that despite the increasingly irritating habit of Tideman in ostentatiously pointing his index finger away each time he called 'out'.

As the Americans held in any frustration they might have been feeling they maintained a supreme composure to save four match points at 5–4 as the tension mounted and the atmosphere became palpably knife-cuttable.

Serving to save a fifth match point at advantage Sundstrom, Witsken thundered a cannonball straight down the centre line. Sundstrom's lunging return sailed out but as it did so the Tideman index finger twitched to where the serve had landed and then pointed away, accompanied by his now familiar cry of 'out'.

If umpire Rosmarin hoped simply to call 'game, set and match' for the Swedish pair, he had another think coming. On the basis that what's held in must come out, Anger finally lived up to his name and exploded dramatically. Or, as *The Times* so quaintly put it, 'the Americans queried the veracity of the call'.

Anger and Witsken insisted the serve was good. The Swedes seemed affronted that their word had been doubted. Amid heated debate Rosmarin was obliged to get down from his chair to make a close examination of innumerable marks in the grey clay as index fingers were used to the full to identify 'the one'.

With no linesmen to consult it soon became a case of third-party intervention by proxy as the American crowd played jury. As more officials piled on to court a voice from courtside yelled, 'It was well in' while another reasoned loudly, 'Why did he return it if it was out?'

For a full ten minutes they were at it as the Swedes spread their arms like fishermen to make their point. First it was three inches out, then at least a foot. Even the Marx Brothers' most anarchic scenes were feeble by comparison.

Finally Rosmarin succumbed to crowd pressure and over-ruled to call the serve 'good'. But if the vote of the arbiter in the skies counts for anything the Swedes must have been right because back at deuce they produced two superb top spin returns and it was all over.

As the quarrelsome youngsters trooped off and the press headlines yelled 'EXPERIMENT ENDS IN PROTRACTED ARGUMENT', beleaguered officials were already muttering, 'Back to square one.'

BACK FROM THE DEAD

WIMBLEDON, JUNE 1983

Although a number of the Wimbledon staff over the years claim to have heard the sound of tennis balls being hit on the Centre Court when it was empty, there is no positive proof of a tennis ghost.

The nearest to it, though, is surely the charismatic Indian player Vijay Amritraj whose story provides one of the most light-hearted episodes in the canon of strange matches.

Vijay's striking good looks couldn't help him win matches but they were certainly no handicap when it came to his ambitions to appear in the movies. Having landed a role in the film *Octopussy*, as sidekick to Roger Moore's James Bond, it suited him just fine that the gala première was being held in London just prior to the 1983 Wimbledon Championships in which he also hoped to star.

Basking in his moment of glory he got together a party of tennis players to take along to the première. They were in a fun mood although one of the group, American Bruce Kleege, was a little down-hearted as he had just missed out on qualifying by the skin of his teeth. His computer ranking made him first reserve should anyone have to drop out.

The players were suitably amused at the Amritraj antics as he swashbuckled his way through a chase sequence swatting villains with his racket. If it had to be him or Bond who bit the dust though, Vijay would take the short straw. While smoothie Roger Moore smiled benignly through to the end Vijay was

220

killed off before the credits.

At the moment of his demise a member of the audience jumped up. It was Bruce Kleege shouting at the top of his voice, 'I'm in! I'm in!'

While the tennis players creased up with laughter, the rest of the star-studded gathering looked at the crazy Yank with pitiful bewilderment.

A few days later Amritraj survived little longer on court than he had done on screen. The only 'ghost' ever to play Wimbledon was obliterated 6–3, 6–4, 7–6 by Australia's Mark Edmondson in the first round.

A FINAL CALL

FLUSHING MEADOWS, NEW YORK, SEPTEMBER 1983

There's a tinge of humour about many of the bizarre incidents in tennis history but sadly not this one. It is arguably the most tragic on-court case in the entire first-class game.

As the 1983 US Open reached its climax, the Flushing Meadows crowds lucky enough to get tickets for finals day on Sunday 11 September had every reason to look forward to a memorable day's tennis.

With the legendary veteran American Jimmy Connors, already four times champion, facing his Czech-born compatriot Ivan Lendl, yet to win the title, great headlines seemed guaranteed one way or another.

So too in the ladies', where another Czech-American, the all-conquering Martina Navratilova, would win her first US title if she could overcome six-times champion Chris Lloyd, a perennial all-American favourite then nearing the veteran stage. Whoever the winner the pressmen would again have a great story.

Yet such is the unpredictability of tennis that a shadow was cast over both matches, and indeed the whole tournament itself, by events in the junior girls' singles final. And it was to be the concrete surface that played the most macabre role.

The record books confirm the bare facts. Connors added a fifth and last US crown to his haul by beating Lendl 6–3, 6–7, 7–5, 6–0 while Navratilova took the first of her four titles in

222

sweeping aside Lloyd 6–1, 6–3. In the girls' singles, 15-year-old Californian Marianne Werdel was beaten by the Australian E. Minter 6–3, 7–5.

Each of the matches was memorable for the winners, and the two main encounters did get the biggest headlines, but it was the match between Werdel and Minter that provided the most indelible record.

Sixty-year-old linesman Dick Wertheimer, from Lexington, Massachusetts, had officiated in enough matches to have been hit a few times. It was an occupational hazard, and taking a blow from a ball always provided amusement for the crowds. This day was no different from any other, so when he took a direct hit in that tender region decorously described by the press as 'the groin area', one couldn't begrudge the barely stifled laughter of the crowd.

But on this day it lasted a mere second. The *Guardian* reported with due gravity that 'Mr Wertheimer was hit in the groin by a ball, fell off his chair, fractured his skull on the "asphalt" court and suffered a heart attack on the way to hospital. Doctors say he is in a critical condition.'

Family, friends and the caring sectors of the tennis community hoped for better bulletins over the next few days but Dick Wertheimer had made his last ever call. He died within days of the freak accident.

It is both one of the strangest and most tragic incidents ever to occur on a tennis court and, ironically, if the US Open had still been played on the old grass at Forest Hills, the outcome might have been happier.

Next time a player decides to bawl at a linesman for a bad call maybe they should be asked to count to ten and remember Richard Wertheimer, who died in the line of duty when he received the call from which there really is no way back.

THE RALLY FROM HELL!

RICHMOND, VIRGINIA, SEPTEMBER 1984

With serves booming down at nearly 150 mph in the men's game and awesomely powerful women like Venus Williams hitting devastating strokes from all quarters of the court, lawn tennis twenty-first century style is a wham-bam game like it's never been before.

'What happened to the stroke play and long rallies of yesteryear?' moan the purists. They've been consigned to the annals of *Tennis's Strangest Matches*, that's what – and thank goodness for that. Unless you're a fan of terminal boredom, that is.

It was the British lady Phyllis Satterthwaite who started it all back in 1930. One of her contemporaries described her as 'an extraordinarily tenacious player who, without appearing to have a winning shot in her game, could always wear down her opponents with lobs of uncanny accuracy and a real fighting spirit.'

Unfortunately she met her Italian counterpart Lucia Valerio in the final of the ladies' singles at Bordighera on the Italian Riviera and so determined was each player to take the title that playing safe took hold of them with a vengeance.

High over the net sailed the ball, straight down the middle too. Playing for the lines simply wasn't an option. Lengthy rallies came thick but certainly not fast and matters reached a head on match point.

The dogged Phyllis duly clinched it after a rally of an

224

astonishing 450 strokes. The pressmen (at least those who hadn't fallen asleep or slipped out for a reviving snifter) immediately dubbed it 'the longest rally in the world'. Never to be broken?

Fast forward to Richmond, Virginia, 25 September 1984, when Vicky Nelson-Dunbar met Jean Hepner. Drilled by their coaches never to hit a 'wasted ball' these players simply didn't know the meaning of the terms 'outright winner' or 'unforced error'.

A score of 6–4, 7–6 to Nelson-Dunbar sounds fairly normal but the match lasted a mind-numbing 6 hours 31 minutes, which included a rally of 643 strokes, still listed as the longest in recognized tournament play.

Just as well they had the tie-break to bring a quick end to their marathon – at 13–11 it was over in a mere flash at 1 hour 47 minutes, with one single point taking 29 minutes to resolve.

One shudders to imagine what junior girls might get up to, notorious for their play-safe approach and without the power to put one away. Shudder no more, but pay homage instead to two gutsy 11-year-olds from La Jolla, California who slugged (or maybe patted) it out in the Anaheim Junior Championships on 13 November 1977. When pint-sized Cari Hagey lost the first set 6–2 to her equally diminutive rival Colette Kavanagh she knew she must dig in at the start of the second set.

Colette, though, was determined not to yield. The mind-boggling result was an opening point of 1,029 strokes which lasted 51½ minutes before Colette won it when Hagey put the ball into the net. The set, which started at 10.30 am, finally finished at 2.05 pm as Miss Hagey took it 6–4 to level up.

In the third she romped home 6–2 and the girls finally shook hands after just over five hours play.

One just has to be thankful that this sort of thing could never happen in the men's game where sooner or later someone always powers a straight winner. Unless, that is, the players happen to be named Ken Phelan and Dr Richard Cohen, who on 23 June 1981 met at the Cynwyd Club in the Philadelphia Clay Court Championships.

In a best of three sets match, Phelan was up 6–1, 5–3 and at match point. Both players had had difficulty hitting winners on the ultra-slow clay and Phelan figured a drop shot might clinch it for him. He was absolutely right, but why he took 29 minutes 25 seconds to have the courage to play it, nobody knows.

Those who were there estimate the ball crossed the net 2,095 times. That's not official, but let's say it was quite a long rally. Utterly unbelievable but just as utterly true!

'Enough is enough,' do I hear you cry? 'Please won't somebody serve an ace?'

So next time anybody moans about a game with too few strokes, just remind them of these rallies from hell. It's true that sometimes the best things come in small packages.

JUST ONE MORE GAME

LAFAYETTE, LOUISIANA, MAY 1985

One of the many great things about a game of tennis is that it needn't be a marathon. Fancy a quick hour at lunchtime or after work? No problem. Forget golf, four hours round the course and the same in the bar afterwards. Not to mention cricket, the lazy man's way of pretending to be busy for an entire day while actually doing very little at all.

Then again, one must confess that even the gentle pursuit of lawn tennis has been known to reach somewhat alarming clock-busting extremes of its own once in a while.

Britain's Roger Taylor must surely have been late for his supper when he beat Poland's Wieslaw Gasoriek in a King's Cup match in Warsaw in 1966 but then what could he expect if he didn't have the game to kill his opponent off quickly? Scores like 27–29, 31–29, 6–4 could see a man starve to death.

And the Americans are more incorrigible still. Put a pair of Richards on court and it seems anything can happen. At the Newport Casino Invitation Tournament in Rhode Island in 1967, Dick Leach and Dick Dell could have settled for a quick second-round exit against fellow Americans Len Schloss and Tom Mazur when they lost the first set 6–3, but they would insist on coming back.

Their 49–47 score in the second was the longest ever set in tennis history.

But were they satisfied? Not while Roger Taylor's 126-game match in Warsaw still held the record for the greatest

227

number of games ever. Everyone knows that the good old US of A always has to go one better so they naturally took the match with a third set score of 22–20 to up the games record to 147.

Of course the introduction of the tie-break in 1970 put a cap on that particular record but that didn't stop another American, John McEnroe, deciding he'd opt for the duration record instead.

His win over Sweden's Mats Wilander in a quarter-final Davis Cup tie in St Louis in 1982 may not sound too excessive at a mere 8–7, 6–2, 15–17, 3–6, 8–6 but they were, it can't be argued, on court a staggering 6 hours 32 minutes in that memorable fifth and deciding rubber.

Such matches do have one thing in common apart from their marathon nature. They were all in serious competition.

Playing tennis for fun is an entirely different matter. After all, who in their right mind would want to play for more than a couple or three hours at a stretch?

Mark and Jim Pinchoff, that's who. They didn't seem to realize that questions of that sort are posed strictly in a rhetorical spirit. Why else would they have started knocking up on court in Lafayette, Louisiana, on 14 May 1985 and carried on playing until the 19th? They were on court 117 hours!

All that remains to be said in the face of such apparent lunacy is that if you fancy setting a tennis record in your neck of the woods, then the very friendly people at the *Guinness Book of Records* will point you in the right direction.

It is a fact, never forget, that to be a serious record-breaker one does need to be fully certified.

KEEPY-UPPY

SANTA BARBARA, CALIFORNIA, MARCH 1988

Thirty-eight-year-old hospital physician Ron Kapp had a specialist interest in the effects of prolonged exercise on the human body.

Marathon tennis, in particular, was something that had always taken his eye. It had the potential, he felt, to have definite aerobic benefits on the way the body functioned.

Such was his interest that he resolved to write a scientific paper on the subject for a medical journal. But Kapp also had his eye on getting into the *Guinness Book of Records*, and so too did his colleague Will Duggan, aged 41.

It seemed the obvious solution to use themselves as the guinea pigs in the experiment. Both were good enough at tennis to put on a decent show and they reckoned that an attempt at the world's longest rally might be their forte.

There had been astonishingly long rallies in tennis matches before, but this was to be a conscious attempt at 'keepy-uppy'. It must, though, said the Guinness people, be part of a full match.

Thus was played, in the unglamorous confines of the Municipal Stadium at Santa Barbara, California, on Saturday 12 March 1988, one of the most remarkable tennis matches of all time.

That the 41-year-old went on to beat the younger man 6–2, 3–6, 7–5 after their extended opening rally might have been a surprise, but hardly mind-numbing. That their marathon rally lasted 3 hours 33 minutes is rather more impressive.

One thing that Dr Kapp might have learned from his scientific experiment is that sooner or later, no matter how good the players, someone has to make a mistake. In the event, it was he who fluffed a forehand but Kapp and Duggan had set their record.

As long rallies go, 6,202 shots is pretty good 'keepy-uppy'.

OH I SAY!

MELBOURNE, AUSTRALIA, JANUARY 1990

Instances of bad player behaviour are legion, hence a policy of selectivity for *Tennis's Strangest Matches* in which only the corkers are allowed entry. Do come in, John Patrick McEnroe.

That this German-born Irish-American New Yorker was a tennis genius is undisputed. Four US Open singles titles, three Wimbledon Championships, three Masters successes and five World Championship Tennis victories are just the pick of the crop.

Equally undisputed is that he was the perpetrator of some of the worst on-court behaviour the game has ever known.

Forget 'You cannot be serious!' and 'Pits of the world'. Those two famous superbrat lines are mere quaint examples of Olde Englishe compared to the verbals that rent the air in Melbourne in 1990.

The scene is Flinders Park, since renamed Melbourne Park. It is Sunday 21 January, the Australian Open. Thirty-year-old John McEnroe, playing with all his old flair, prepares to meet Sweden's 26-year-old Mikael Pernfors in the fourth round, on Centre Court. McEnroe seems relaxed coming into the game and expects to win.

But those expectations are about to be reversed, and in the most shameful manner possible.

McEnroe took the first set 6–1 but Pernfors had chances and McEnroe seemed to realize this, becoming edgy, disputing a couple of calls and whining about photographers moving

231

during points. Umpire Gerry Armstrong and official courtside supervisor Ken Farrar knew the signs. These preliminary volcanic rumblings could lead to a major eruption. Better be on guard.

In the fourth game of the second set Pernfors broke serve aided by a close call from a lineswoman, then held to go 4–1 up. Changing ends, McEnroe walked towards the lineswoman and stood just a couple of feet away, repeatedly bouncing the ball on his racket. He said nothing, but glared long and menacingly.

The English umpire Armstrong tried to nip things in the bud and issued a warning for 'intimidation'. That was step one in a Code of Conduct which had just been altered from four steps to three. Pre-1990 it was warning, point penalty, game penalty and default but step three, the game penalty, had just been eliminated. McEnroe did know this, but it had slipped his troubled mind.

Pernfors won the second set. In the third a baby cried in the stands and a few fans yelled 'just shut up and play' when McEnroe himself began to yelp, but he kept his composure to take the set 7–5.

Two sets to one ahead. No cause for alarm. Serving at 2–3 and deuce in the fourth McEnroe pushed a forehand wide. Annoyed with himself, he hurled his racket to the ground. The crack was clearly audible. So too was the umpire's warning. 'Racket abuse Mr McEnroe. Point penalty.'

One step from disqualification, but McEnroe thinks he still has two lives. The point penalty gave Pernfors the game for a 4–2 lead so McEnroe argued the toss.

'You broke the racket,' Armstrong told him. 'That's automatic, John.'

'All I did was crack it,' whined McEnroe. 'I have every intention of continuing to play with it.' This was splitting hairs and Armstrong simply said 'Let's play,' a sort of unwritten code for a final warning.

McEnroe, still miscalculating, didn't take the hint and demanded to see referee Peter Bellenger. The umpire also signalled for supervisor Ken Farrar, who held the real power.

McEnroe repeated the spurious racket-cracking argument. Farrar, Armstrong and Bellenger listened patiently but remained unmoved. This time it was Farrar who said 'Let's play.' Maybe he should have said 'Let's pray.'

Farrar turned for the tunnel. McEnroe knew he had lost the argument. Still thinking he had two warnings left he made the worst decision of his career and let fly with a parting shot.

He could have said, 'Man, you're the pits.' Maybe even, 'You stink, Farrar.' Both would have brought disqualification with dishonour, but perhaps an acceptable degree of dishonour, if that is possible. McEnroe chose neither of these phrases.

With apologies to the very young or particularly sensitive, for I 'must' quote McEnroe verbatim, what he did shout in a rather loud voice was 'Just go fuck your mother!' Oh dear.

An Australian television audience of millions watched aghast as commentator John Alexander told viewers that McEnroe had 'just used a terrible profanity'. Farrar turned on his heels and having confirmed with the umpire that his hearing was fine, retribution was swift. 'Verbal abuse, audible obscenity, Mr McEnroe. Default. Game, set and match Pernfors.'

McEnroe stood hands on hips, a stunned smile on his face, but the game was up. It was the first time a top-ranked player had ever been evicted from a major tournament.

Bearing in mind the manner of its occurrence, it would not be an exaggeration to say that in Melbourne at 5.30 pm on Sunday 21 January 1990, the game of lawn tennis hit its all-time low.

As this unsavoury affair leaves rather a bitter aftertaste, let's finish on a lighter note. McEnroe was by no means the first player to be disqualified from any tournament. Here's a last word from Nicholas Lane Jackson, the Ken Farrar of the 1890s:

At St Servan in France in 1891 I had a most unpleasant experience. I had arranged for one of our best players, a delightful woman, to play with an Englishman of some repute, but who was noted for a somewhat uncontrollable temper. During their mixed, the umpire rather offended this man, who disgusted the spectators and terrified his partner by knocking every ball he could find into an adjacent garden. After seeing two dozen balls disposed of in this fashion the secretary appealed to me so I went to the court where I found the game at a standstill and the lady in tears. As my reprimand only evoked a rude reply I had no choice but to order the game to be awarded to the other side. The curmudgeon who packed up and left that same evening never did forgive me.

CASTLE'S RED CARD

TELFORD, NOVEMBER 1990

If anyone had asked Andrew Castle to pay £2,400 for a piece of brown cardboard measuring 12 inches × 8 inches his answer certainly wouldn't have been printable in *Tennis's Strangest Matches*. Yet that is precisely what a piece of cardboard did cost the defending British title holder in the final of the Prudential National Championships at Telford on Sunday 4 November 1990.

Davis Cup player Castle was a solid enough player but never in the really big-money league. Maybe that's why this rather outspoken red, known on the circuit as 'the raging socialist', wasn't altogether keen on the newly introduced property tax which had been the subject of so much debate. The infamous poll tax smacked too much of medieval serfdom for Castle's liking.

Not that the ordinary man could make a stand, Castle knew that. But our Andrew was no ordinary man so, knowing that the British Championships were being televised live for the first time, he decided to stage a one-man protest of his own.

NO TO POLL TAX said his cardboard sign plonked in full camera view next to his chair during changeovers. His opponent Jeremy Bates, known affectionately to Castle as 'the fascist', remained entirely unmoved by his red-shirted opponent's demo. But less calm about the matter was tournament referee Colin Hess. It was after the fifth game of the first set that he asked Castle to remove the offending notice, only for the player to respond by asking to see the rule that he'd breached before reluctantly putting it aside and producing another which read HELLO, MUM, IN TAUNTON.

Surely he wasn't extracting the proverbial from the LTA? Concentrating on the tennis might have been a better option, because as well as a £9,600 first prize the victor gained automatic entry into the following week's Diet Pepsi indoor challenge at Wembley, a tournament which included US Open champion Pete Sampras and would potentially pay Castle's poll tax bill in Merton many times over.

Alas, he who lives for the cause must sometimes die for it, as Castle found to his cost, slumping to a 6–3, 6–2 defeat in 80 inglorious minutes. As 'the fascist' picked up the £9,600, Castle allowed himself a wry smile as he pocketed the £4,800 loser's cheque, but it was a smile that didn't last long.

The LTA were not amused, promptly banning him from playing for Britain in the European Cup and fining him a pocket-wrenching £2,400.

'It was just a little joke,' pleaded Castle. 'I've already paid my poll tax. I'm hurt and very angry. The judgement is harsh and I shall appeal.'

But the LTA were on the warpath. A political demonstration was the last thing they needed in the midst of negotiations for a new sponsor. The appeal was summarily dismissed.

Perhaps worse for Castle was that he was forced to issue a contrite apology. And not only that – a quick-thinking BBC producer had cut all the shots of the offending placard so no one outside the Telford metropolis had got the message. That begs the question 'Is Telford the centre of world political activism?' We might as well ask 'Will a British lady win next year's Wimbledon?'

It was the day 'the fascist' beat 'the raging socialist' and *The Times* rubbed it in with the headline 'BATES HAS LAST LAUGH ON CASTLE'. At a cost of £25 per square inch of plain old cardboard it's difficult to argue with that one – but no doubt Andrew Castle did.

The poll tax, meanwhile, duly bit the dust. And these days Andrew Castle, enjoying his career change as a Breakfast TV presenter, gets his message to the millions in a very different way.

TRUTH STRANGER THAN FICTION

HAMBURG, APRIL 1993

'The world's number one lady tennis player, just 19 years old and carrying all before her, is stabbed on court by a crazed fan of her leading rival in front of thousands of spectators and a TV audience of millions.'

This is, surely, the blurb from one of those tawdry tennis novels which Ilie Nastase and Martina Navratilova would insist on writing. An utterly ludicrous plot that simply wouldn't happen in real life. Except that it did.

As Yugoslavian-born Monica Seles prepared for the Citizen Cup in April 1993, the next event on the Women's Tennis Association tour, she had every reason to be supremely confident.

She had won seven of the previous nine Grand Slam tournaments and become the then youngest ever number one ranked player in tennis history. Hitting fearsomely powerful double-handers off both sides, delivered with her trademark grunt, Monica appeared simply unstoppable. Even the German star Steffi Graf seemed destined to accept number two slot for some years to come.

Monica's quarter-final against Bulgaria's Magdalena Maleeva on Centre Court at Hamburg's Rothenbaum Club promised to be routine fare but a 7,000 crowd were packed in to see the world champion.

It was 6.49 on Friday 30 April as the players changed ends. Monica trailed 4–3 in the first set after being 3–0 down but would surely, as ever, complete the comeback.

A minute later, as she left her courtside chair to go out to serve, a dishevelled-looking man suddenly sprang from the stands and stabbed her in the back with a kitchen knife just below the left shoulder blade.

As the star slumped to the floor, tour director Lisa Gratton and courtside helper Carsten Maleesa rushed to her aid. Their initial impressions were ones of relief: the half-inch wound was not life threatening. It later required just two stitches.

But the haunted look on Monica's face said it all and, as she was rushed by ambulance to the University Clinic hospital, the psychological effects had already begun. The wound would heal quickly but she would not have the confidence to play again for a full 27 months.

The 38-year-old East German Gunther Parche, an unemployed lathe operator from Thuringen, explained to police that he never intended to kill Seles, merely to stop her playing for a while so that his idol Steffi Graf could retain the number one ranking. The most deranged fan in the game's history got his wish. Steffi took top slot on 7 June.

Astonishingly, due to the vagaries of the German legal system and a very clever lawyer, Parche later left the law courts a free man. The judge asserted that he was 'not a serious danger to anyone else'.

When Seles returned to action on 29 July 1995 in an exhibition match against Martina Navratilova in Atlantic City, the world's press saw her win 6–3, 6–2: 'She marked her comeback with a double fault,' said the *Sunday Telegraph*, 'but once she got going, those lacerating ground strokes and passing shots had Martina flailing at air.'

The best quote came from Monica herself. Asked about her comeback after the match she smiled once again and simply said: 'This whole thing for me has been, like, wow!'

In truth, though, she has never been quite the same again. Nor has tennis, with bodyguards now *de rigueur* for the top stars.

The remarkable Hamburg stabbing incident is one affair which even an avid tennis strangeologist must hope is never surpassed.

LADIES AND GENTLEMEN, NO FLASH PLEASE

ROLAND GARROS, PARIS, MAY 1994

Nothing much phased the aggressive American Jim Courier. Blistering strokes from either side and an intense competitiveness had won him plenty of titles and he arrived at the 1994 French Open as winner in 1991 and 1992 and runner-up in 1993.

He had been struggling with form, it's true, hence his lowly seeding of seven in 1994, but he wasn't expected to have too much trouble against French hopeful Jean Philippe Fleurian in the first round. The Paris mob, though, had other ideas as they crowded into the brand new Court A on Tuesday 24 May.

But all the cat-calling in the world couldn't put Courier off his stroke as he brushed the Frenchman aside 6–1 in the first set and moved ominously ahead in the second.

Then something seemed to distract him. He looked uncomfortable and when he served an astonishing seven consecutive faults he seemed positively flustered. In true Courier fashion, though, he pulled himself together to take the set 6–4 and finished off the match to record a score of 6–1, 6–4, 6–4.

A bland, uneventful score if ever there was one, but only afterwards did the shocking truth behind Courier's mid-match blip emerge. One of Monsieur Fleurian's female fans, it seems, had decided to take matters into her own hands – or rather legs.

The Times reported the matter with as much delicacy as they could muster and even printed a picture of the long-haired brunette concerned: 'Courier's concentration had been broken by the activities of a female,' they said, 'who was seen occasionally to give him a shout, upon which she would part her legs, raise her skirt and show her knickers!'

Only when a couple of burly security men moved in to sit either side of her did the free show stop. After a short chat she admitted that her flash may have distracted the American player; it was, after all, an open and shut case.

Unsubstantiated rumours later circulated that the knicker-flash version of events reported by *The Times* was, strictly speaking, inaccurate, largely because the offending items had been noticeable by their absence.

So, was she or wasn't she?

Apart from the lady herself, perhaps only Jim Courier, who ended his Parisian experience runner-up to Spain's Sergei Bruguera, knows the answer to that delicate question.

PADDLE TENNIS

MELBOURNE, AUSTRALIA, JANUARY 1995

'It was hard to tell whether André Agassi looked more like the Pirate King, Sinbad the Sailor or Popeye,' wrote Alan Trengrove in *Australian Tennis Magazine* in 1995 after he had seen the Las Vegas-born 24-year-old bludgeon his way through the field to win the Australian Open at his first attempt.

Maybe Agassi knew something nobody else did because in his semi-final against fellow American Aaron Krickstein, his newly adopted seafaring style certainly ended up looking more appropriate than anyone could possibly have predicted.

Turning up at Melbourne's magnificent Flinders Park (now Melbourne Park) wearing gold earrings in both ears, a bandana and sporting a goatee-style beard certainly made Double 'A' look like something that had wandered in from the set of a *Peter Pan* movie, but the high-seas look hardly seemed appropriate for an antipodean summer at a stadium where play had been known to have been suspended on the grounds of it being too hot.

That's not to say that the Australian Open hadn't known rain before. Indeed, when the pressure built up, heavy tropical storms were apt to erupt, but that sort of natural phenomenon couldn't scupper the organizers at Flinders Park because they had a major secret weapon of their own up their sleeve.

Their famous retractable roof over the stunning centre court meant not even the heaviest rain could dampen their spirits.

As the crowd settled for the start of the Agassi–Krickstein semi on Friday 27 January 1995 they had every reason to believe they'd see a full-length match with no unforeseen weather problems. In the event they were wrong on both counts.

Some rain had already been forecast so the roof was closed prior to the start of play. Agassi captured the first set 6–4, a set in which Krickstein tweaked a groin to add to the hamstring injury he was already carrying. Obviously affected but hanging in there, Krickstein again limited Agassi to 6–4 in the second as rain began drumming down relentlessly on the roof above.

As the crowd willed Krickstein to keep going as he trailed 3–0 in the third, the fact that they had been denied a classic was at least balanced by the knowledge they'd cheated nature, so often the tennis killjoy. If the Agassi game finished quickly there would surely be another match scheduled.

Five minutes later hopes were shattered on both fronts. As the sky was lit by an almighty lightning flash and the faintest trickle of water had begun to creep into one corner of the court, Krickstein decided he could no longer carry on because of the injury. Maybe he foresaw the deluge that followed.

As the crowd applause rippled and the players began to leave court, ripples of a more watery kind seemed to be getting larger. Had the unbreachable roof failed? No. But where there's a will, there's a way.

The elements cunningly decided to attack from below and seep up from underneath the court. Within five minutes of the players' departure the entire court was under water and play was abandoned for the day.

'It soon rose to knee-height,' stated *The Times* under the masterful headline 'AGASSI TIDE ROLLS ON AS KRICKSTEIN REACHES LOWEST EBB'.

'Dozens of people, including Wimbledon ladies' champion Conchita Martinez, went paddling in the instantly created pool,' added the *Guardian*.

There have been tennis floods but never one quite so unexpected or impossible as this one. All was revealed to the equally soggy press shortly afterwards as many reporters perched atop desks marooned in the state-of-the-art pressroom which had also meekly succumbed.

The lightning had caused a partial power failure which shut down the pumping equipment that usually conveyed surplus storm water into the River Yarra adjacent to the grounds. As pressure in the drains intensified a number of them simply blew and opted to disgorge themselves on Centre Court.

'You would think that with a roof over the stadium, you've got all the angles covered,' mused Agassi, 'but I hope the court is dry for Sunday and it's going to be fun.'

It was and it was. 'Pistol Pete' Sampras was made to walk the plank as Agassi triumphed in four sets.

SHAME OF A NATION

WIMBLEDON, JUNE 1995

There is something in the character of the British tennis fan that makes them particularly responsive, in a restrained and rather nervous way, to unexpected happenings.

The gentle titter which ripples its way around a Wimbledon court on the occasions when such events are 'amusing' may be a nation's half-stifled acknowledgement that decorum has been momentarily and involuntarily pricked, for it is not matched anywhere else in the world.

We all know the sort of thing.

In 1963, a canine intruder held up the men's singles game between J. E. Sharpe and J. W. Frost on No. 3 court; on the opening day in 1998 it was a mouse, which fancied a closer look at Centre Court and which had to be ushered off in the match between Yevgeny Kafelnikov and Mark Philippoussis. Trainee kamikaze pigeons regularly conduct test flights on No. 1 Court. All such incidents score highly, not least because they involve living creatures which large sectors of the British public appear to hold in much higher regard than many of the players.

But just once in a while it all goes horribly wrong and an unexpected incident draws a collective gasp of shocked disbelief, none more so than at Wimbledon in the early evening of Wednesday 28 June 1995 on Court 14.

To grasp the enormity of this sorry affair three things need to be understood. The British love of all things feathered or

244

furry is only matched by their motherly attitude towards Wimbledon ballboys and ballgirls, who have an 'Aah!' factor all of their own.

This in turn is only superseded by the nation's undying love of the British players, perfectly epitomized in 1995 by their growing affection for the promising 20-year-old Oxfordshire boy Tim Henman. Tall, dark and handsome and from a tennis family in which his great-grandmother and grandfather had both played at Wimbledon, Henman was the perfect model of Britishness and carried the nation's hopes on his young shoulders.

Thirdly, in the 118 years since the first Wimbledon in 1877, no player had ever been disqualified from the Championships. The stage is set.

It was the first round of the men's doubles. The British pair Tim Henman and Jeremy Bates faced the Swede Henrik Holm and his American partner Jeff Tarango. As the closely fought battle reached a tense tie-break in the fourth set, with the score at 7–6, 2–6, 6–3, 6–6 in the British pair's favour, Henman momentarily lost his cool after losing a crucial point.

Scooping up a ball, he glanced down court to check the coast was clear, and gave it an almighty thwack.

Now the Wimbledon ballgirls are well drilled and quick on their feet. Too quick for Tim Henman. As he drew back his racket, 16-year-old Caroline Hall was already on the way across the net gathering up a wayward ball. She took the full force on the ear, gunned down by Tim's speeding yellow bullet, but crumpled to the ground only for an instant before showing true British pluck and continuing her run as the tears flowed.

Had it been an overseas player, the crowd's boos would have been deafening. But this was a tricky one to call, an own goal of head-holding magnitude.

Umpire Wayne McEwan did call it, though, and after a short consultation with referee Alan Mills, Henman and Bates were defaulted. As a British player became the first ever to be disqualified from Wimbledon, the crowd greeted the decision with a befuddled mixture of boos and dumbfounded amazement.

Caroline Hall recovered fully but the British press had their say. 'DISGRACED TENNIS BRAT' and 'BAD BOY TIM', screamed the morning headlines. For Henman and his family it was undoubtedly a public humiliation: 'I remember coming in the next day and it was as if I'd murdered someone,' he later recalled.

A nation's character had surely been sullied. There was, it seemed, no way out but to grin and bear it.

It was then that Henman delivered his master stroke, issuing a public apology delivered with a kiss and a huge bouquet of flowers. White lilies, a spray of purple and plenty of greenery. A nation gasped yet again . . . the Wimbledon colours. There was even a small roundlet of yellow blooms peeking out from the gypsophila, surely a representation of the errant ball.

Caroline Hall was quoted in Friday's press: 'It was a complete accident. I was unlucky, as was Tim. He has said sorry but I had already forgiven him. I know he didn't mean to hit me.' It was masterly damage limitation and the sort of photo opportunity the tabloids can't resist. Pictures of a smiling Tim and Caroline were everywhere.

Tennis matches can certainly be strange. But there is nothing so strange as human nature. Again Henman recalls: 'I had to deal with the press at their most evil. Then I took the ballgirl some flowers and I was the nicest guy in the world.'

It was one of the great escapes of tennis and there is a curious postscript which made it stranger still. Although he was fined £1,910, Henman's disqualification was all but forgotten three days later when one of his doubles opponents, Jeff Tarango, became the first man to be disqualified from the singles.

And he didn't say it with flowers.

MUCH ADO ABOUT NOTHING

WIMBLEDON, JULY 1995

Tennis can be wonderfully dramatic. William Shakespeare's works were not made complete without him serving up several references to the ancient game along the way. Alas, lawn tennis came around 250 years too late for the Bard to have his way with it, which is a pity, because what drama, tragedy and comedy might have been inspired by one Jeff Tarango.

This 26-year-old Californian arrived at Wimbledon with a pretty unimpressive record. Although ranked 80 in the world he entered the hallowed grounds of SW19 with a Wimbledon baggage of six successive first-round defeats and the loss of 18 consecutive sets. The home of tennis evidently didn't suit him.

He also brought with him his French wife Benedicte and a reputation for dodgy behaviour. Verbal abuse was habitual for Tarango and in 1994 he had shown crowds in the Land of the Rising Sun an entirely different aspect of the solar system when he dropped his shorts for a full moon after losing his serve in a defeat by Michael Chang in Tokyo. 'People say tennis is boring and I just lost my head,' he explained. 'My shorts came down and the gig was up.'

Wimbledon held its breath. Tarango broke his nightmare sequence and advanced to the third round to play Germany's Alexander Mronz. Perhaps he thought this was his year and got himself all worked up, for what was to follow stunned the tennis world.

There were plenty of spectators wedged in around Court 13

on Saturday 1 July as French umpire Bruno Rebeuh called the players to order. He and Tarango already had a history. In fact the player had complained about him so vehemently to the authorities in the past that Tarango believed he had an 'agreement' that Rebeuh would not umpire any of his matches. Their paths hadn't crossed again until now.

Tarango was twitchy but pleased to see his favourite official supervisor at courtside. It was a Wimbledon of glorious sunshine but strangely as the match began the clouds hung low. The temperature, though, was rising.

Tarango lost the first set 7–6. There were minor histrionics but nothing new. Early in the second, with both players in with an equal shout, a Tarango serve, which he thought was an ace, was called out. He had a minor spat with the umpire but looked set to resume when catcalls and slow handclapping from the crowd sent him over the edge.

Tarango ranted and yelled for them to shut up. The umpire issued a warning for an 'audible obscenity'.

'I'm not having that. How come they can say what they want and I can't?' roared Tarango. 'I want the supervisor. I've got a big beef.'

It wasn't an anatomical boast, merely an indication that he was a trifle upset. Then Tarango noticed his favourite supervisor had been replaced by the Swede Stefan Fransson, one not on his approved list. Fransson upheld the warning. Tarango turned on umpire Rebeuh.

'You're the most corrupt official in the game – I'm not playing any more.'

As Rebeuh called a point penalty, Tarango slammed down the two balls in his hand with a yell of 'That's it. I'm not playing – no way' before duly stalking off court amid thunderous boos and jeers.

It was an automatic default at 6–7, 1–2 and Tarango, described by the *Guardian* next day as 'the pasty-faced Yank', became the first ever man to be disqualified from the Wimbledon singles in its 109-year history.

It might have ended there but, as the umpire made his way back to the sanctuary of his office, Mrs Tarango landed an almighty slap across his face before joining hubby in the press conference.

It was an absolute riot. Even hardened hacks were outraged: 'That guy needs help,' yelled one American. 'Do you have a persecution complex?' inquired a polite but perplexed English voice. There was no remorse: 'I'm so glad you did that,' Tarango told his wife, before reviling Rebeuh for bias to French players and a long-running campaign against himself.

And so it went on. All excuses, no apologies.

The English public tut-tutted as only they can: 'It's just not cricket,' they cried. It wasn't tennis either, not as we know it. The papers had a field day. 'LAST TARANGO IN SW19 AS OFFICIAL IS ATTACKED', blasted the *Guardian*.

The general conclusion was that the poor chap was deranged. Surely he didn't think he was going to 'win' Wimbledon, for goodness' sake. He was provisionally banned from his next Grand Slam event and the following year's Wimbledon and conditionally fined £10,000.

Tarango had affronted the tennis world and a second-rate third-round clash on Court 13 entered the game's history.

Not content with making a complete fool of himself, Tarango, a student of philosophy, confirmed his inhabitation of a fantasy kingdom in which he was the sole ruler, by approaching the tournament referee Alan Mills on the eve of his journey back to the States.

Mills later related the story not knowing whether to laugh or cry: 'Tarango came up to see me and said: "I don't suppose there's much chance of me getting my prize money tonight, is there?"'

It was the only thing poor Jeff ever got right at Wimbledon.

SINGIN' IN THE RAIN

WIMBLEDON, JULY 1996

A quarter-final match between Dutchman Richard Krajicek and three-in-a-row Wimbledon champion Pete Sampras always promised much but no one could have predicted such a stirring response as that given by the *Guardian* when it was all over: 'Something magical happened in Centre Court on Wednesday 3 July, an event in its own way every bit as much a testament to the fortitude of the native British spirit as Elizabeth I's rallying of the troops against the Armada some years back.'

Yet bizarrely it wasn't the tennis that made this match so strangely memorable, but what happened when the rains came and the tennis stopped.

At a Wimbledon already badly interrupted by inclement weather, the last thing a troubled referee and the increasingly fractious crowds wanted was a wet Wednesday. But they got it all the same. After play began at 12.30, games were just 2–all in the first set when the heavens opened yet again. Three hours later, with the green covers raised tent-like over the court, it was still bucketing down.

Sandwiches had been eaten, books read, crosswords finished and British resolve tested to such limits that the bedraggled crowd were beginning to look mighty glum.

Enter Sir Cliff Richard, the Peter Pan of Pop, an avid regular at the Championships.

'Would he, perchance, be prepared to deliver a song or two

to raise the flagging spirits of the Centre Court faithful?' ventured a Wimbledon official. Cliff answered in the affirmative and it was just like the war all over again.

Appearing in the royal box with a microphone, the 55-year-old icon began his repertoire with, naturally, 'Summer Holiday'. With unwavering eccentricity the British fans cast off their dampened spirits and joined in.

'The Young Ones' swiftly followed. Then 'Bachelor Boy' and 'Livin' Doll'. As the scene became ever more surreal, Sir Cliff was joined by a backing group including Martina Navratilova, Pam Shriver, Gigi Fernandez and one-time Queen of All England Virginia Wade. 'The Supremes!' quipped Sir Cliff as the many foreigners in the crowd looked on in puzzled astonishment.

As the crowd swayed in time to the ditties and Cliff danced with a black lady corporal on royal box security duty, the unthinkable happened. The sun came out and resumption of play was announced.

Cliff left the stage with a cheery 'I never thought I'd play the Centre Court' and Sampras and Krajikec resumed battle once more. Most of the crowd present that day forget that, between further rain breaks, they saw Krajicek take a two set to love lead before a further shower finally curtailed play just after 8 pm at 1–1 in the third.

Being one of those days, even that fate came courtesy of a Wimbledon oddity as it was a delay in covering the court that finally drew the curtain on this unpredictable affair. Ground staff member Mark Hillaby failed to follow the drill, ending up in hospital after tripping and banging his head during the attempted cover up.

For the record, Krajicek later prevailed over Sampras and went on to win his first Wimbledon crown, but it was Cliff who was that year's star.

His impromptu turn was surely the best Centre Court performance by a British man since Fred Perry completed his hat trick of wins in 1936.

The man of the moment was duly acknowledged in the annual *Wimbledon Compendium*, bible of the Championships, by the following entry in which one word might more kindly have been omitted: 'During a prolonged spell of rain on the second Wednesday, Sir Cliff Richard entertained the Centre Court spectators by singing many of his *old* songs.' Ouch!

A WINNING STREAK

WIMBLEDON, JULY 1996

The apparent obsession of the All England Lawn Tennis and Croquet Club with the state of dress or undress of competitors was completely put in the shade on the sunny afternoon of Sunday 7 July 1996 when someone employed within the very grounds of the club itself finally went all the way.

A touch of ankle, no stockings, shorts for women, shorts for men, mini-dresses, halter-neck tops; thus progressed over the years the gradual erosion of dress-code 'decency' so highly valued by Wimbledon's self-appointed arbiters of good taste.

By the time Miss Anne White of the United States took the all-white rule to its logical conclusion by appearing on Court 2 in 1985 in a figure-hugging, neck-to-ankle white body-suit there was surely little left for the players to try.

Miss White, by the way, was censured for her action as, to coin a phrase first used by the Wimbledon authorities in 1949 over the Gussy Moran panties saga, her costume 'drew too much attention to the sexual area'. Anne agreed to cover up, later musing, 'I didn't want to put anyone off their straw-berries and cream.'

So what next? Competitors playing naked? Not even Wimbledon were yet fearful of that one, but as a good second best there had been talk for a number of years of the likelihood of streakers defiling the sacred greensward.

Ever since Michael O'Brien had his embarrassment covered by a policeman's helmet in a rugby match at Twickenham in

1974, sport had experienced a streaking epidemic. In 1982 Erica Roe bounced on to the scene, again at Twickenham, and since then no sport has been safe. Cricket leads the way but even the more theatrical setting of snooker and the sedate conservatism of bowls have been hit.

No one had dared to try it on Wimbledon's Centre Court, but prior to the 1996 Championships William Hill bookmakers were offering just 4–1 on a streaker interrupting Centre Court play during the men's final. It was almost bound to become a self-fulfilling prophecy, although when it did the spectacle was reserved only for the match preliminaries.

Men's final, Sunday 7 July 1996. Fourteen thousand spectators on Centre Court and a packed royal box. Finalists Richard Krajicek and Mali Vai Washington pose for photographs at the net prior to warm-up.

Enter 23-year-old blonde London student Melissa Johnson, taking a break from her summer-holiday catering duties in the grounds to leap over a barrier and run the length of the court wearing just a minuscule maid's apron. Sporting a huge smile, Miss Johnson lifted her apron to give both players an eyeful and then proceeded to do likewise for the royals before being led away by a gentleman of the law.

Would the royals be offended? The Duke and Duchess of Kent and Prince and Princess Michael of Kent were visibly amused. Seventeen-year-old Lord Frederick Windsor looked as if he hadn't enjoyed a tennis match so much for years and the knock-up hadn't even begun.

As for the players, they laughed too. Mali Vai Washington walked back to the baseline to begin his warm-up, lifted his shirt to reveal his bare chest and received a huge ovation.

The streak was, in its way, both the most sensational and remarkably unsensational event in Wimbledon's 119-year history. All over in a flash and scarcely an offended soul to be found.

The club that had held its breath filled with dread for so long issued a formal statement: 'Whilst we do not wish to condone the practice, it did at least provide some light amusement for our loyal and patient supporters, who have had a trying time during the recent bad weather.'

Melissa was taken to Wimbledon police station for the duration of the final and released without further action.

As for the match itself, we mustn't forget, although most people do, that Krajicek became the first Dutchman to win Wimbledon, sweeping aside the unseeded American 6–3, 6–4, 6–3 in 94 minutes.

It was the day the Wimbledon ice was finally and irredeemably broken, and everybody cried Bravo! Even the beaten finalist shrugged his shoulders and gave a disarming interview: 'I look over and see this streaker. She lifted up the apron and she was smiling at me. I got flustered and three sets later I was gone; that was pretty funny,' said Washington, clutching his loser's cheque for £196,250.

Serious lawn tennis historians may wish to consult the excellent photographic work *Visions of Wimbledon* published by André Deutsch.

COURT JESTER

ALBERT HALL, LONDON, DECEMBER 1997

London's magnificent Albert Hall, famous home to countless musical performances, has also hosted many tennis matches. Its circular tiered arrangement gives it an air of gladiatorial combat and its sheer Victorian splendour surely makes it the most opulent tennis venue of all time.

But it isn't the unusual setting that qualifies a match played there in December 1997 for strange status. It's the presence of one Mansour Bahrami, court jester par excellence.

His match against Bjorn Borg for the third place play-off in a popular Seniors Tour event wasn't one of world significance. Just a chance for the audience to see quality players the wrong side of 40 still strutting their stuff. Bahrami lost it 6–1, 5–7, 10–1. The odd score in the final set was the first to ten points 'champions tie-break' used as a deciding set in such contests.

As a match it was unmemorable. Yet everybody there *would* remember it, quite simply because Mansour Bahrami is the most entertaining tennis player of all time and any one of his matches would send the 'strangeometer' right off the scale.

Consider his repertoire: A ball hit through his legs is as routine as a volley played behind his back. Serving with six balls in his hand is no big deal. Sometimes he hits them all at once. His viciously spun backhand drop shot can be unreturnable, not least because when he gets it really right it bounces back over the net whence it came.

Retrieving a succession of smashes with a series of

'moonballing' lobs is a trademark but it's tiring work. Bahrami's answer as he's forced deeper and deeper beyond the baseline is simple. He sits in the linesman's chair and lobs from there, subject to just a touch of directional co-operation from his opponent.

His cannonball serve forces his opponent way behind the baseline. That is until Bahrami winds up for a really big one, swishes and misses deliberately and before the ball hits the ground delivers a legitimate under-arm backhand serve just over the net. The forward-lunging fall guy at the other end seldom gets there in time.

A ball caught in his pocket, returns played with either hand, or well-observed take-offs of some of the tennis greats might be slipped in for good measure. Tennis is never dull when Mansour Bahrami takes to the court.

Yet strange as his game undoubtedly can be, especially on the exhibition circuit, perhaps equally strange is the hidden side to Bahrami's life that few of his applauding and giggling gallery are ever aware of.

Born in Arak, Iran, on 26 April 1956, he first learnt the game by watching others as a ballboy at a club in Tehran. His father earned a pittance as a gardener and the whole family lived in a single room. Affording a racket was beyond young Mansour's dreams, so he practised with a dustbin lid or a piece of wood in the street. A kindly member of Iran's Davis Cup squad gave him a racket when he was 12, but when he tried to get a court at the local club he was roughly shown the door by a bullying security guard.

Overcoming such prejudice, he made the Iran Davis Cup team at 17 but the Islamic revolution of 1979 strangely resulted in a ban on tennis and all courts were closed for three years.

Bahrami fled to Paris but, hampered from entering tournaments by onerous restrictions on Iranian passport holders, his promising career was massively disrupted. Yet he became a good enough player to rank 192 in the world and make the doubles final at the 1989 French Open.

Make no mistake. Bahrami is a clown of the first order but

257

certainly no fool and behind the antics delivered with a twinkle in the eye and a twitch of the walrus moustache, is an excellent lawn tennis player with a life story straight out of fiction.

Which just goes to show that sometimes the off-court facts are as strange as the on-court action.

KERSHAW'S TENNIS VISION

KINGSTON-UPON-HULL, APRIL 1998

The connections between the historic port of Hull and the noble art of lawn tennis are hardly legion, but one player has ensured that the town better known for its rugby teams has secured a place in *Tennis's Strangest Matches*.

This is the remarkable story of the sports science student, the radio DJ and a dog named Bonnie.

When 26-year-old Hull College student Sarah Kershaw decided to take up tennis in September 1997 no one seemed too enthusiastic. Although she'd followed the game avidly through the media for years, even her parents didn't back her ability to play.

So, determined to prove all and sundry wrong, Sarah set to and formed her own club at the Kingston Park Tennis Centre.

That might seem a heavy-handed way of going about things but for Sarah it was really the only option. Her promotional GET VIT campaign was aimed firmly at aspiring players just like Sarah and, in such a manner, Visually Impaired Tennis arrived in the UK.

So intrigued by the campaign was local Viking Radio DJ Scott Makin that he challenged Sarah to a match in April 1998. She promptly beat him.

'For me it's like tennis in the dark,' explained Sarah. 'I'm seriously visually impaired and all I see over the net is a cloudy blur of my opponent. I can just detect which side they're hitting on and from there can pick up a faint flight of the ball.'

After experimenting with yellow football-size sponge balls, Sarah settled for regular tennis balls coloured bright pink: 'I'm allowed two bounces,' she explained, 'and because my ears are very sensitive I listen out for the sound of the ball and can pick it up on second bounce if I'm quick enough.'

Trust and sportsmanship is a great part of VIT because either a sighted opponent or independent supervisor makes the line calls. One of Sarah's greatest supporters proved to be her guide dog Bonnie, a constant courtside companion and enthusiastic impromptu ballgirl.

Maybe the critics that say tennis is all about power and money have never visited Kingston Park Indoor Tennis Centre. Nor have they ever witnessed the remarkable skills and manoeuvrability displayed by players on the flourishing wheelchair tennis circuit. Or seen a young lad with an artificial leg hit a blistering forehand down the line.

Sometimes the strangest games are also the most inspirational.

IT ALL ENDED IN TEARS

ROLAND GARROS, PARIS, JUNE 1999

Martina Hingis was born to a life in tennis. When her mother Melanie Molitor, a Czech champion, won a tournament in the summer of 1980 she was already pregnant. When the baby arrived on 30 September she was named Martina after Czech-born legend Martina Navratilova.

Serious coaching began when she was two and by the age of 12 she was the youngest ever winner of a junior Grand Slam event when she took the 1993 French Open by storm.

But a return visit to Paris six years later was memorable for very different reasons. In some of the strangest scenes ever seen on court in the ladies' game, Martina threw the wobbler of all time.

Living in Switzerland and dubbed by the press 'The Can't Miss Swiss', the young prodigy had swept all before her. In March 1997 she supplanted Steffi Graf to become the youngest world number one and, when she arrived in Paris for the 1999 French Open, had five Grand Slam titles and over 100 weeks as number one under her trim little belt.

Impressive stuff. But some critics said the immense pressure and a suspect attitude would catch up with her. It would, they said, all end in tears. They were right.

In the final of the French at Roland Garros Stadium on Saturday 5 June, 18-year-old Hingis faced 29-year-old Steffi Graf. The French Open was the only Grand Slam to have eluded Hingis. Graf had already won it five times. Hingis was desperate for victory. She believed passionately that her time had come.

Although admired by most tennis fans, cracks had begun to appear in the smiling Hingis façade some months earlier. Describing muscular French newcomer Amelie Mauresmo as 'half a man' at the Australian Open wasn't a good idea. Nor were her snipes when she split with doubles partner Jana Novotna. She reportedly dismissed the reigning Wimbledon singles champion as 'too old and too slow'. People began to wonder what lay beneath the sugar-sweet coating.

In Paris they remembered and started to barrack right from the second round in which Hingis beat the very 'half a man' of her thoughtless derision. Nor had Hingis endeared herself to all the players on tour; one anonymous lady pulled no punches in asserting 'a lot of us see her as a cocky little madam who thinks she's someone really special'.

Hingis started the final well but apparently tetchy, taking the first set 6–4 but incurring a warning for racket throwing. At 2–0 in the second she seemed to be coasting to her first French title. On the first point of the third game her driven forehand return was called out.

Adamant that it had dropped in, which TV later supported, Hingis broke the rules by marching round to Graf's side of the net to highlight the mark in the clay. As umpire Anne Lasserre remained unconvinced, Hingis planted herself in a chair and called for the referee. The crowd jeered, the referee arrived and promptly gave her a point penalty for unsportsmanlike behaviour, just one step from automatic defaultment.

The *Guardian* described her attitude as 'entirely reprehensible'. The crowd agreed, prompting more sympathetic TV commentator Frew McMillan to observe, 'They're baiting her.'

The second set slipped from her grasp 7–5 after she had served for the match at 5–4. In the third, looking increasingly distraught, she took a five-minute toilet break and there were murmurings she wouldn't reappear. When she did she culminated her dramatic Act One with what the *Observer* described as 'a performance of emotional immaturity that ill served both herself and her sport' by twice serving underarm on match points.

Much to the delight of the 16,000 crowd Graf easily prevailed to take the set 6–2, but Act Two of the Hingis drama was still to come.

Instead of shaking hands and waiting for the trophy presentation she rushed off court to her waiting mother, later pushing the Women's Tennis Association communications director who had the temerity to ask for an interview.

When she did come back, one highly respected newspaper correspondent observed, 'She sobbed uncontrollably on her mother's shoulder and sat in the umpire's chair before delivering a brave but unhappy little speech to cap her impression of a two-year-old in the midst of a lost dummy wobbly.'

And that was one of the kinder remarks. Hingis remained unrepentant and claimed to be 'misunderstood': 'I don't think my behaviour today was too bad,' she mused. 'I guess I'm too difficult to understand because when I play it looks so easy. I basically can do whatever I want with the ball.'

Damage limitation it wasn't and two weeks later, when she crashed out of Wimbledon 6–2, 6–0 to qualifier Jelena Dokic, itself one of the strangest tennis results of all time, that statement came back to haunt her and the press again got the knives out.

There has never been a stranger display of public petulance from a lady star than on the June day in Paris when Martina's 'want it all, have it all' world finally betrayed her.

Equally strange, but very telling too, was the unprecedented vitriolic character assassination pursued by the press and the fact that many genuine tennis fans loved every bit of it.

But then the masses have always enjoyed public executions, especially in Paris.

A CRUCIAL BREAK

MONTE CARLO, APRIL 2000

When you have the fastest timed serve in the world, solid ground strokes and the advantage of years over your older and lower-ranked opponent, you don't expect to have to resort to creative excuses for losing. But that's exactly what Britain's Canadian-born adopted son Greg Rusedski did when he crashed out of the Monte Carlo Open in the first round in April 2000.

The French Riviera has been one of the most idyllic places to play tennis ever since the late nineteenth century but when tenth-seeded Rusedski met the Czech player Slava Dosadel on Monday 17 April unseasonal rain delayed proceedings.

Perhaps the deluge was providential for later it was an unscheduled one of a natural but altogether different kind that Rusedski blamed for his early exit.

The British number two struggled from the start. With his serve not fully functioning he lost the first set 6–4. In the second he came back from the brink as with Dosadel serving for the match he broke serve and took the set 7–6 after a convincing 7–3 tie-break. One set all. A deciding third to come.

The slow and heavy clay had taken its toll and the 29-year-old Czech looked tired. Rusedski prepared to close out the match. It was then that Dosadel played his master stroke, taking advantage of the prevailing rules to take a 'toilet break'.

As bad calls go, this call of nature seems to have upset

Rusedski more than most. He was promptly hammered 6–1 when Dosadel, evidently much relieved, reappeared on court.

Now the average trip to the gents is a pretty rapid affair. Did Dosadel get lost? His little bit of off-court business took ten whole minutes.

Although Rusedski conceded he'd not played well he made it equally clear that he wasn't impressed with Dosadel's bladder control: 'I wasn't happy about that ten-minute toilet break,' he whined. 'It frustrated me. I could see he was really tired and just sitting in the cubicle is a good idea. I had him down and out. I don't know about you but when I go to the loo it doesn't take me ten minutes.'

It's either the lamest excuse of all time or the shrewdest piece of tactical skulduggery ever employed. Whichever side one chooses to support, it enabled the *Daily Mail* headline writers to have some fun at Greg's expense.

He surely must have flushed at 'RUSEDSKI HOPES GO DOWN PAN'.

THE ROYAL COMMAND PERFORMANCE

BUCKINGHAM PALACE, LONDON, JULY 2000

The 1980 Wimbledon final between 'Superbrat' John McEnroe and the Swedish 'Ice Man' Bjorn Borg was a true classic. Although Borg won the match to clinch an astonishing fifth Wimbledon singles title in a row, it was the amazing fourth-set tie-break that many people remember to this day. McEnroe saved seven match points before taking it 18–16.

When the two players staged a charity re-match 20 years later on Sunday 2 July 2000, it was no classic but it was certainly one of the most unusual matches of all time.

When the players were first approached by a patron of the National Society for Prevention of Cruelty to Children they were very positive. But when Wimbledon refused to stage the match and other venues didn't come off, the event seemed in doubt.

Indeed, McEnroe and Borg might well have called it a day when the patron came up with a brainwave that sounded rather like desperation.

'There's a tennis court in my mother's garden,' he said. 'We could use that if she's willing.' Despite taking a month to decide, Mum agreed to let the back garden host the event. But would the players agree?

A definite 'Yes' in unison was the swift answer. The patron was Prince Andrew, His Royal Highness the Duke of York. Mum was Queen Elizabeth II. The back garden was part of the 36 acres of Buckingham Palace.

The press had a great time in the hyped build-up: 'BIG MAC'S ON PALACE MENU', punned the *Daily Mail*. In fact it was champagne and Arctic sea bass that the celebrity guests dined on at the pre-match luncheon. Then by way of entertainment they were treated to a specially arranged changing of the guards ceremony, quickly followed by a song from legendary performer Art Garfunkel.

Never had a single tennis match been blessed with such a star-studded audience. All eyes might have been on tennis's 'Russian Babe' Anna Kournikova, but for the fact that immediately in front of her sat film star Liz Hurley, and a few seats away supermodel Claudia Schiffer. Eyes on stalks were much in evidence.

Grand Prix legend Damon Hill and golfing giant Nick Faldo, too, normally turn heads, but just a few yards away sat Prince Andrew, his former wife Sarah and the two princesses Eugenie and Beatrice.

And so it went on. Not an ordinary punter in sight. 'People's Sunday' it wasn't. The players might almost have been extras. While McEnroe exclaimed, 'I can't believe I'm here,' the Ice Man kept his customary cool. In fact he was just a bit too cool as, during the match itself, 44-year-old Borg struggled to hit form. He was evidently very fit but on the superslow asphalt court simply couldn't generate pace.

Blessedly a much-mellowed McEnroe behaved himself. What else could he do with Eastbourne umpire Gerry Armstrong in the chair, the very man who ten years before had defaulted him from the Australian Open. If 'Mighty Mouth' had said this day what he said that day he'd surely be in the Tower of London now, and I'd be in the dungeon next to him for daring to report it.

But of course there were some high jinks. McEnroe complained during the knock-up: 'They told me it was going to be on grass.' Later when he tripped on the sticky tarmac surface he turned to the Duke of York and threatened, 'You'll be hearing from my lawyer.'

It was all what was expected for a showbiz crowd.

In truth as a match it was a cruel parody of their game 20

years earlier. Rain interrupted proceedings before McEnroe ran out easy winner 6–3, 7–6. This time the tie-break was instantly forgettable as McEnroe quipped: 'The older we get, the better we used to be.'

A strange encounter it certainly was. A time-warp game in a fantasy setting watched by more millionaires than one cares to imagine. And, to cap it all, the match raised a record £1.5 million for the NSPCC.

It remains to record just one more oddity. Observing the pre-match toss, the TV commentator was moved to remark on its appropriateness as it came up heads.

This was the only match in tennis history in which the owner of the court had gone to the trouble of having her portrait engraved on the coin. Now that's style, ma'am.

DID DAD CALL THE SHOTS?

WIMBLEDON, JULY 2000

Despite overcast skies on most days, Wimbledon's Millennium Championships proved the brightest for some time as story after story made the headlines.

None was more hyped than the semi-final clash between black American sisters Venus and Serena Williams, the first ever occasion on which sisters had met for a place in the Wimbledon final.

But, unusual as the statistic is, it isn't that which qualifies the match for 'strange' status. Nor is it the girls' unusual route to stardom. Growing up far from privilege in the Compton ghetto district of south central Los Angeles, they were taught the game by their father Richard, who schooled himself in the rudiments by buying a 'how to do it' book and video when he decided that tennis was the route to riches for his girls.

Way before they reached their teens he was declaring both would be champions. Richard Williams was a man with a mission.

Younger sister Serena won the US Open in 1999. As their semi-final showdown loomed, 20-year-old Venus had yet to land a Grand Slam title.

Most experts tipped Serena to win on form alone but even before the match some respected observers in the know, including players, were already imbuing the contest with its status as an oddity in tennis history.

The result, they said, would be contrived. Dad would give

Serena 'orders' to lose. It was, quite simply, Venus's turn.

Even though Serena had been hitting even hotter than Venus in the run-up, veiled predictions were rife. Reigning champion Lindsay Davenport felt Venus would win 'for outside reasons'. The 1961 runner-up Christine Janes, British to the core and naturally opposed to skulduggery of any kind, puzzled her fellow *Radio 5 Live* commentators with the mysterious assertion that the match, which promised to be an all-time classic, would be 'flat'.

She was spot on. On Thursday 6 July Venus duly romped to victory, 6–2, 7–6.

Some of the papers were quick to say Serena 'lost' it. The *Daily Mail* pulled few punches: 'The Williams sisters upset the formbook and sparked a conspiracy theory to rival the assassination of JFK yesterday as hot favourite Serena blundered her way to semi-final defeat,' it said.

That sort of talk sparked much debate. Camps became split. The match was dissected.

Eighteen-year-old Serena had bludgeoned her way to the semis by dropping only 13 games in five matches en route. Against big sister the unforced errors came thick and fast as she lost another 13 games in this one match. The first set sailed by but, when Venus served two double faults in the first game of the second, a real contest looked on.

Both sisters hit flat out as Serena eased ahead 4–2 and the expectant crowd anticipated a deciding set. Was that the point at which 'Dad's orders' kicked in? Serena promptly lost 11 points in a row, including 5 unforced errors. She trailed 5–4.

Games went to 6–all and a tie-break. Serena led 3–2 before losing the final five points and finishing on a limp double fault.

It was all over. Venus walked sadly to the net, looking rather bemused and concerned and without a flicker of her famous winning smile. Serena fought back tears.

Naturally enough the media asked all the right questions: 'Was it a family carve up? Had Father issued orders?' it probed. 'Not as far as I'm aware,' replied Venus, with what seemed like a very genuine response. Serena somewhat guiltily cast down her eyes and simply said, 'I can't answer that question for my family.'

The tennis psychologists drew their own conclusions. Little sister had gone the way of younger siblings the world over, reluctantly accepting to the point of tears that 'father knows best'.

The headline writers punned themselves silly: 'THE SISTERS PLAY UGLY AND SAD SERENA MISSES THE BALL,' barked the *Daily Mail*.

Only Serena will ever know whether the unforced errors were genuine. What does remain certain is that two days later, Venus beat Lindsay Davenport and lifted her first Grand Slam trophy with such an unbridled display of spontaneous joy that the tennis world was uplifted.

Two days later again the sister act once more hit Centre Court and Serena was back to form as the Williams pairing bounded unfettered to the ladies' doubles title.

Richard Williams was already on his way home. Both his girls were champions. Mission accomplished.

NO STRINGS ATTACHED

BRIGHTON, NOVEMBER 2000

Goran Ivanisevic arrived at the Samsung Open in Brighton with a reputation as one of the game's most interesting characters. Whether it was his bullet serve, fiery temper, famously gloomy moods or his frequent threats to quit the circuit, the giant Croatian had always been a bit of a one.

Even on good days they called him 'Ivan the Terrible'. On bad ones he was 'Ivan the 'Orrible'.

Some said he was mellowing with age but those present at the Brighton Indoor Centre on Thursday 23 November saw Goran write a unique chapter into the story of his eventful career.

Without a title since 1998 and his world ranking in free fall at 134th, the former Wimbledon finalist entered Brighton with high hopes. A weak field gave him a great chance and a second-round match against South Korea's Hyung-Taik Lee didn't seem to present too much of a problem to Ivanisevic.

How wrong could he be? It proved to be a smashing game but one in which he made history for all the wrong reasons.

Things started to go awry in the first set when he dropped his serve to go 6–5 down. As a response he promptly smashed his racket, flinging the mangled frame into a bin with great ceremony as umpire Kim Craven announced a code violation for racket abuse. Lee kept his cool and his racket to take the set 7–5.

Ivanisevic recovered his composure to take the second set

7–6 after a tie-break and entered the deciding third determined not to crack. Unfortunately, after letting two break points slip by at 1–1, it was racket number two that did the cracking after a hefty blow on the baseline.

Ivanisevic persevered with it until the next changeover before dumping that one, too, in the bin. Down in games 2–1, down in rackets 2–0.

Four points later a double fault presented Lee with two break points and at 15–40 down Ivan again succumbed to the sudden urge to enter the world of racket redesign. The red mist descended and he smashed his third on the floor, receiving a point penalty which cost him the game.

Things then took an even odder turn. Ivanisevic told umpire Craven that he'd run out of rackets. Tour supervisor Gerry Armstrong and tournament referee Alan Mills (why is it *always* those two?) were called to the scene.

'Gerry, I have no more rackets,' said Ivanisevic with all the pathos he could muster.

'Tough,' replied Armstrong, or words to that effect. There was no alternative but for the racketless Croat to retire forthwith.

'Ladies and gentlemen, due to lack of appropriate equipment, game, set and match Lee, 7–5, 6–7, 3–1' announced umpire Craven, trying his best to stifle an involuntary smirk.

Having smashed three rackets in one match Goran Ivanisevic became the first player in history to retire in such a way.

'Now I will go home and maybe get some new rackets for Christmas,' he said, 'but if I feel like I do now I will probably break them too.'

Even 124 years into lawn-tennis history, strangeness still comes calling in new guises. That's why 'Ivan the Terrible' left the Brighton tournament the most empty-handed loser of all time.

Selected Bibliography

Aberdare, Lord, *The Willis Faber Book of Tennis and Rackets*, 1980

Amritraj, Vijay, *Vijay*, 1990

Ashe, Arthur, *Portrait in Motion*, 1975

Barrett, John, *World of Tennis*, 1969

Barrett, John, *100 Wimbledon Championships*, 1986

Borg, Mariana, *Love Match: My Life with Bjorn*, 1982

Brady, Maurice, *The Centre Court Story*, 1956

Burrow, F. R., *My Tournaments*, 1922

Chipp, Herbert, *Lawn Tennis Recollections*, 1898

Cleather, Nora, *Wimbledon Story*, 1947

Clerici, Gianni, *Tennis*, 1976

Collins, Bud, *Encyclopedia of Tennis*, 1980

Deford, Frank, *Big Bill Tilden*, 1976

Evans, Richard, *Open Tennis*, 1988

Evans, Richard, *The Davis Cup*, 1998

Forbes, Gordon, *A Handful of Summers*, 1978

Forbes, Gordon, *Too Soon to Panic*, 1995

Frayne, Trent, *Famous Women Tennis Players*, 1979

Freddi, Cris, *The Guinness Book of Sporting Blunders*, 1994

Heathcote, J. M. and C. G., *Tennis, Lawn Tennis, Rackets, Fives*, 1903

Jackson, N. Lane, *Sporting Days and Sporting Ways*, 1932